TheatreUpClose presents
the world premiere of

A TALE
OF TWO CITIES

adapted for the stage by
Terence Rattigan and John Gielgud
from the novel by Charles Dickens.
Edited by Adam Spreadbury-Maher.

The production opened at the King's Head Theatre
on 25 September 2013.

THEATREUPCLOSE

Cover photograph by Christopher Tribble
Used by permission of TheatreUpClose

ISBN 978-0-573-11437-3
Printed in the United Kingdom

Published in 2013 by Samuel French

UNITED STATES AND CANADA

Samuel French, Inc., 45 West 25th Street, New York NY 10010
info@samuelfrench.com
1-866-598-8449

UK, EUROPE AND REST OF WORLD
Samuel French Ltd, 52 Fitzroy St, London W1T 5JR
plays@samuelfrench-london.co.uk
0207 255 4315

For all other rights, apply to: Alan Brodie Representation, Paddock Suite, The Courtyard, 55 Charterhouse Street, London EC1M 6HA

WWW.SAMUELFRENCH-LONDON.CO.UK
WWW.SAMUELFRENCH.COM

A TALE OF TWO CITIES

adapted for the stage by Terence Rattigan and John Gielgud
from the novel by Charles Dickens. Edited by Adam Spreadbury-Maher.

SYDNEY CARTON	Stewart Agnew
JARVIS LORRY	Paul Beech
CHARLES DARNAY	Nicholas Bishop
MADAME DEFARGE	Shelley Lang
LUCIE MANETTE	Jennie Gruner
MISS PROSS	Flaminia Cinque
DOCTOR MANETTE	John Hodgkinson
JERRY CRUNCHER	Giles Stoakley
DIRECTOR	Adam Spreadbury-Maher
SET DESIGNER	Christopher Hone
COSTUME DESIGNER	Jonathan Lipman
LIGHTING DESIGNER	Seth Rook Williams
CASTING DIRECTOR	Sophie Holland
ASSISTANT DIRECTOR	Chloe Mashiter
FIGHT DIRECTOR	Zoe Swenson-Graham
PRODUCTION MANAGER	Louisa Davis
STAGE MANAGER	Giles Stoakley
DEPUTY STAGE MANAGER	Toby Gauntlett
ASSISTANT STAGE MANAGER	Kristina Jackson
PRODUCERS	Dominic Haddock
	Rachel Lerman
ASSOCIATE PRODUCER	Dan Leach
ASSISTANT PRODUCERS	Liz Aspinall
	Lianne Bloeman
PUBLICITY	Amanda Malpass PR
GRAPHIC DESIGN	Design by Minty
SOUND DESIGN	The 27 Club

Stewart Agnew

SYDNEY CARTON & MARQUIS

Stewart has just graduated from East 15 Acting School. *A Tale of Two Cities* will be his first professional production. His credits while at East 15 include Sydney Carton in the production of *A Tale of Two Cities* earlier this year, Oswald Mosely in *Blackshirts*, Polonius in *Hamlet*, Angelo in *Measure for Measure*, Vanya in *Uncle Vanya*, Writer in *Vieux Carré*, David in *After the Dance*, Lnt Jacobs in *Oh! What A Lovely War*, DeFlores in *The Changeling*, Macbeth in *Macbeth* (for the Sam Wanamaker Festival at the Globe) and Stella in *The Sidcup Family Portrait* (for Caligula's Alibi Theatre Company).

Paul Beech

LORRY, JUDGE & ROADMENDER

Most of Paul's forty-year-long acting career has been in theatre, starting at the Gateway Theatre in Chester back in October, 1973. He has appeared in numerous other provincial repertory theatres, including Cheltenham, Chesterfield, Coventry, Derby, Mold, Northampton, Sheffield, Sheringham, Southwold, Watford, Westcliff and Worthing. Tours in plays and musicals have taken him to many other theatres over the years. He has also appeared at the English Speaking Theatres in Vienna and Frankfurt and has toured to the Genting Highlands in Malaysia. Roles have included Roat in *Wait Until Dark*, Harvey Bunker in *Season's Greetings*, Sir Antony Absolute in *The Rivals*, Daniel Peggotty in *David Copperfield*, Sol Gill in *Dombey and Son*, Dr. Wangel in *The Lady from the*

Sea, Eliot Chase in *Private Lives*, Sir Peter Teazle in *The School for Scandal*, Mr. Brownlow in *Oliver* and the title role in *King Lear* in last year's production by Sir Jonathan Miller. West End appearances have included *The Mousetrap*, *Liberace's Suit* and *The Last Confession*.

On screen, he appeared as Charles Dickens in *Mr. Dickens Presents*, introducing and taking part in scenes from five of the author's novels, and a series of commercials advertising Ferrero's Gran Soleil which took him to Italy thirteen times.

Most recently, he played Laertes, father of Odysseus, in a promenade production of *The Ithaca Axis* which took audiences to a variety of locations in Bristol varying from Red Lodge to the underground caves in Redcliff.

Nicholas Bishop

DARNAY & DEFARGE

Nicholas most recently starred in *Moby Dick* at the Arcola Theatre as Starbuck having previously taken on the role of Harcourt in Polly Findlay's *The Country Wife* at the Manchester Royal Exchange. Other theatre includes: *The Guinea Pig Club* (York Theatre Royal), Captain Nicholls in *War Horse* (National Theatre), Peter in *The Railway Children* (Waterloo Station), Froth in *Measure For Measure* (Plymouth Theatre Royal), Longavillie in *Love's Labours Lost* (Rose Theatre), Bottom in *A Midsummer Night's Dream* (OUDS), McMurphy in *One Flew Over The Cuckoo's Nest* (Oxford Playhouse), Romeo in *Romeo and Juliet* (Old Firestation Oxford), Tom in *Skylight* (O'Reilly Theatre Oxford), John in *Oleanna* (Burton Taylor Studio), Otto in *Design For Living* (Old Firestation Oxford), Various roles in The Oxford Revue (Oxford Playhouse), Danny in *Sexual Perversity in Chicago* (Burton Taylor Studio), Sebastian in *Twelfth Night* (Old Firestation Oxford), Cornelius in *Jail Talk* (Burton Taylor Studio), Brian in *A Triple Bill Of Shame* (Greyfriar's Kirkhouse, Edinburgh Festival).

Television includes: Ferdinand in *Doll & Em* (Revolution Films), Giacomo in *Cranford* Season Two (BBC), Agent Chambers in *The Cell II* (Sony/Fox/Endemol) and Jake Stafford in *Banged Up Abroad* (Raw TV).

Flaminia Cinque

MISS PROSS, SOLICITOR-GENERAL, GABELLE & SEAMSTRESS

Training: Cambridge Footlights. Bristol Old Vic Theatre School.

Theatre includes: *The Permanent Way* (also Sydney Australia) by David Hare and *The Neighbour* by Meredith Oakes (National Theatre), *The Rose Tattoo* by Tennessee Williams, *Lysistrata* by Aristophanes (and Epidavros), *Mind Millie For Me* by Feydeau and *Portrait of a Lady* (Peter Hall Company); *The Late Henry Moss* by Sam Shepherd and *Measure for Measure* (Almeida Theatre), *The Glass Menagerie*, *The Winslow Boy*, *French Without Tears*, *Othello*, *The Respectable Wedding* by Brecht, *More Grimm Tales* (also New York and Sydney) by The Brothers Grimm (Young Vic London), *Push Up* (Royal Court Theatre).

Television includes: *Any Human Heart*, *Ashes to Ashes*, *Fresh Meat*, *Gophers*, *Tinga Tinga Tales*, *The Safe House*, *New Tricks*, *Silent Witness*, *Waking the Dead*, *Doctors*, *The Savages*, *Drop the Dead Donkey*, *Sunnyside Farm*, *Hustle II*, *KYTV*, *Lovejoy*, *Freddie and Max*, *Agony Again*, *Beethoven's Not Dead*, *Supply and Demand*, *Lake of Darkness*, *Blue Murder*.

Film includes: *Bridget Jones – The Edge of Reason*, *The Knot*, *Leap Year*, *Mr Bean's Holiday*, *Attack the Block*, *What a Girl Wants*, *Tezz*, *Ashes and Sands*.

Radio includes: *David Copperfield*, *Dombey and Son*, *Mr Luby's Fear of Heaven*, *What Went Wrong with the Olympics*, *What a Carve Up*, *All the Young Dudes*, *Behind the Crease*, *The Miles and Milner Show*.

Jennie Gruner

LUCIE MANETTE, CHILD & FRANCOIS

Jennie Gruner studied at The Central School of Speech & Drama. Whilst training she was cast as Julia in feature film *Zero* (Sterling Pictures, Dir. David Barrouk, Exec Prod. Nicolas Roeg), due to be released later this year. Other credits include Petal in *Above & Beyond* (Corinthia Hotel, Look Left Look Right, 2013), *Dogs* (Tristan Bates Theatre, 2013), *Press Pass* (Bush Theatre, 2012), *London: Four Corners One Heart* (Theatre 503, 2012), *Seduced* (Dir. Michael Kingsbury), Ellie in Television Comedy Pilot *This is Steve*, and the lead in LSFF short film winner *Come Clean*. She was voted one of the 'Rising Stars of 2013' by The London Magazine.

John Hodgkinson

DR MANETTE & GASPARD

Theatre credits include *A Walk On Part* (Soho Theatre, Arts Theatre), *Behud* (Soho Theatre), *Onassis*, *The Winter's Tale* (Headlong tour), *His Dark Materials* (Birmingham Rep), *Artisto and The Visit* (Chichester Festival Theatre), *Hapgood* (Birmingham Rep/ West Yorkshire Playhouse), *Absurdia* and *The Front Page* (Donmar Warehouse), *Uncle Vanya* (Birmingham Rep), *The Eleventh Capital* (Royal Court), *The Taming of the Shrew, A Midsummer Night's Dream, Romeo and Juliet, As You Like It, Two Gentlemen of Verona* and *Oh! What A Lovely War* (all for Regent's Park Open Air), *A Journey To London* (Orange Tree Theatre), *Neville's Island* and *The Hare Trilogy* (Birmingham Rep), *I Have Been Here Before* (Watford Palace Theatre), *Bov* (Arcadia), *Alice in Wonderland* and *Alice Through The Looking Glass* (RSC), *The Seagull* (RNT).

Television includes: *Big Bad World* (Comedy Central), *The Escape Artist* (BBC), *Whitechapel* (Carnival ITV), *Silk* (BBC), *Holby City* (BBC), *Criminal Justice* (BBC), *Fallout* (Channel 4), *Heartbeat* (ITV), *Broken News* (BBC), *Brief Encounters – All In A Day's Work* (BBC), *Doctors* (BBC), *EastEnders* (BBC), *My Family* (BBC), *Peep Show* (Objective/Channel 4).

Film includes: *Heart of Lightness* (Arnholm), *Leave to Remain* (Indefinite Films), *Skyfall* (B23 Ltd), *Thunder Pants* (Dragon Pictures), *Firelight* (Carnival Films), *Whatever Happened to Harold Smith?* (West Eleven).

Shelley Lang

MADAME DEFARGE & STRYVER

Born and raised in Blantyre, Glasgow, Shelley emigrated to Perth, Australia aged 10. She returned to the UK in 2004 to train at The Poor School in London. Shelley is an Associate Artist of the King's Head Theatre. Theatre includes: La Corbie in the London Premiere of Liz Lochhead's *Mary Queen Of Scots Got Her Head Chopped Off* (King's Head Theatre), Abigail in Arnold Wesker's *Denial* (King's Head Theatre), *Happiness* (Wayfarer Productions, King's Head Theatre), Julie and Lisa in *Cosi* (King's Head Theatre), Jane in the Tennessee Williams World Premiere *I Never Get Dressed Till After Dark On Sundays* (Cock Tavern Theatre - Best Actress Nominee, OffWestEnd Awards), Pippa in the UK premiere of Hannie Rayson's *Hotel Sorrento* (Cock Tavern Theatre), Becky in Nick Ward's *The Present* (Cock Tavern Theatre), Louise in *After The End* (Golden Lion Theatre), Sally in *Elegies For Angels, Punks And Raging Queens* (Workhouse Theatre), Lisa in *The Dice House* (Hen and Chickens), Michael Stewart's *Brood* (The Albany) and *Pizza Man* (Soho Theatre).

TV and film includes: Penrose in *Inception* (Christopher Nolan, Warner Brothers) Daniella Hendry in *River City* (BBC Scotland), *Berry's Way* (BBC), *Sex On Trial* (ITV), *Good As Gone* and *Lullaby* (BBC New Film Making Network Shortlist - Much Mojo Productions).

Further credits: Patrick Bruel's "She's Gone" (music video), You Am I's "Trigger Finger" (music video), The Boy Least Likely To's "George And Andrew" (music video), Mary Boone in Harold Finley's *1000 Miles Of History* (rehearsed reading). www.shelleylang.com

Giles Stoakley

CRUNCHER & BASARD

Giles has played an eclectic mixture of roles in the theatre ranging from Big Bird in an international tour of *Sesame Street* for Premier Stage Productions, to Bottom in an outdoor production of *A Midsummer Night's Dream* for the Festival Players. He has also played a number of other Shakespearean roles including Benedick, Leonato, Friar Lawrence and Macduff, both on tour and in venues such as the Ashcroft Theatre in Croydon. In the last few years he has appeared in a number of more modern theatre pieces as well, including new adaptations of *Wuthering Heights* and *Lysistrata* (again for the Ashcroft Theatre) and a number of pantomimes, most recently playing the Emperor in *Aladdin*. In addition to this Giles works as a voiceover artist, voicing anything from adverts to corporate training manuals. He is currently the voice behind the Boris bikes on the TFL website. Over the last few years he has branched into Stage and Production Management, for touring shows like *Wildboyz the Musical*, and for The Elgiva Theatre's production of *The Wizard of Oz*.

PRODUCTION TEAM

Adam Spreadbury-Maher | DIRECTOR

Adam is an award-winning director and producer, originally trained as a tenor in Australia. Adam founded the Cock Tavern Theatre in 2009 and won the Peter Brook Dan Crawford award. He founded OperaUpClose with Ben Cooper and Robin Norton-Hale, producing *La Bohème* at the Cock Tavern and Soho Theatres, winner of the Olivier Award for Best Opera.

Directing highlights: Louis Nowra's *Cosi* and Daniel Reitz's *Studies For A Portrait* (White Bear), Peter Gill's *The York Realist* and *The Sleepers Den* (Riverside Studios), Hannie Rayson's *Hotel Sorrento* and a new play by Edward Bond, *There Will Be More* (Cock Tavern Theatre), and in Australia Jonathan Harvey's *Beautiful Thing* and Joe Orton's *Loot*. For OperaUpClose he directed *Tosca* (Soho Theatre and King's Head Theatre), *Ballo* (*A Masked Ball*) (King's Head) and *Madam Butterfly* (King's Head).

Producing highlights: Jack Hibberd's *A Stretch of the Imagination*, the hit musical *Pins and Needles*, and the landmark six-play Edward Bond retrospective (Cock Tavern Theatre), *The Coronation of Poppea* and *Someone to Blame* (King's Head) and *Don Giovanni* (Soho Theatre).

In 2010 Adam became Artistic Director of the King's Head and won Best Artistic Director in the Fringe Report Awards. In 2011 he was nominated for Best Director in the Off-West End Awards. Follow him on Twitter @Spreadbury or visit www.spreadbury-maher.com.

Christopher Hone | SET DESIGNER

Christopher studied Theatre Design at Nottingham Trent University.

Theatre includes: *Tosca* (OperaUpClose at Soho Theatre), *Coyote Ugly* and *The Time of Your Life* (Finborough Theatre), *The Lesson, Vincent in Brixton, Romeo and Juliet, A Taste of Honey, Hamlet* and *Othello* (International Tour), *One Minute* (Courtyard Theatre), *Here* and *A Place at The Table* (Tristan Bates), *Gawkagogo Freakshow* (National Tour), *Guerilla/ Whore, Pirates of Penzance, Cinderella* and *Stiffed!* (Tabard), *Dorian Gray* (Leicester Square Theatre), *Gilbert is Dead* (Hoxton Hall) *The Great Gatsby, Quasimodo* and *Starchild* (King's Head Theatre), *Rip Her to Shreds* (Old Red Lion), *Over Here!* (Saban Theatre, Los Angeles).

TV includes: the complete studio re-design of QVC UK Studios, *Big Brother, The Great British Weather, Hollyoaks* and numerous commercials and virals.

Jonathan Lipman | COSTUME DESIGNER

As Costume Designer, recent theatre includes *Tosca* (Soho Theatre), *Purity and Desire* (Drill Hall, London), *The Country Girl* (West End, national tour), *Larkrise to Candleford, Jekyll and Hyde: The Musical, Keeler* (national tours, West End), *La Fanciulla del West, Tosca* (OperaUpClose, King's Head Theatre), *Vieux Carré* (King's Head Theatre, West End), *The Handyman* (Yvonne Arnaud Theatre, national tour), *Quasimodo* (TheatreUpClose, King's Head Theatre), *Ballo* (OperaUpClose, King's Head Theatre), *The Heart of The Matter* (West End), *Pope Joan* (NYT, London).

Film includes *The Houdini Girl*.

As Associate Costume Designer, theatre includes *Richard III* (Old Vic, BAM, world tour); *Dr Dee* (Manchester International Festival, ENO).

Seth Rook Williams | LIGHTING DESIGNER

Seth studied Lighting Design at Wimbledon College of Art. His recent designs include: *Romeo and Juliet* (Leicester Square Theatre) and *The Great Gatsby* (King's Head Theatre and Riverside Studios) with *Ruby in the Dust*; *Tame Game* and *The End is Near* with Bloom! Dance Collective (European Tour); *The Observatory* (Underbelly, Edinburgh Fringe), *The Altitude Brothers* (National Tour) and *Bitch Boxer* (Soho Theatre and National Tour) with Snuff Box Theatre; *Bound* with Bear Trap Theatre (National Tours and Southwark Playhouse); *You and Me* with Little Soldier Productions (RichMix & International Tours); *Where The White Stops* with Antler Theatre and *Boris & Sergey Perilous Escapade* with Flabbergast Theatre at the Edinburgh Fringe 2013, *Vieux Carré* (Charing Cross Theatre), *Quasimodo* (King's Head Theatre) and *Tosca* (Soho Theatre) with Theatre/OperaUpClose. Seth also works regularly at The Place, Euston where he lights various productions for the London Contemporary Dance School.

Sophie Holland | CASTING DIRECTOR

Casting Director for *Pentecost* (OffWestEnd Award Nominee for Best Ensemble) and *SOCHI 2014* (King's Head Theatre). Casting Associate on *Vexed* and *New Tricks X* (BBC), *Dracula* (NBC), *Reign* (CW), and *Outlander* (Sky). Casting Assistant for Channel 4 comedy *Pilot Man Down, Bully Boy* (St James Theatre), *Fleming* (Sky Atlantic), *Strike Back* (Sky), *Life of Crime* (ITV), *Mad Dogs Series 4* (Sky), *Walking On Sunshine* (Vertigo). Children's Casting Associate for *Thor 2 - The Dark World.*

Chloe Mashiter | ASSISTANT DIRECTOR

Chloe is a director and writer whose other assisting credits include *The Suicide* (The Space); *59 Minutes to Save Christmas* (Barbican); R&D for *The Pied Piper* (NT Studio); *A Progress* (The Yard Theatre) and *Much Ado About Nothing* (Cambridge Arts Theatre).

Her directing credits include *The Angel* (Drayton Theatre), *Swindlestock* (Rose Bruford College), *Lonely Hearts Club* (Pleasance Islington), *Envy* (The George Tavern), *You Didn't See Anything* (Lost Theatre) and *Twelfth Night* (Japanese tour). Her writing has featured at the International Student Drama Festival, Open Arts Café, Nice Spread, Lost Theatre and most recently in Riff Raff's Lost Soles season.

Chloe frequently works with Future Cinema, including their recent productions of *The Shawshank Redemption, Brazil, Saturday Night Fever* and the launch of Secret Music. She has also performed at the Edinburgh Fringe, NSDF11 and Latitude Festival. Chloe is a member of the Finborough Theatre's literary team and helped to judge this year's Papatango new writing competition.

Dominic Haddock | PRODUCER

Dominic graduated in Theatre and Performance Studies from the University of Warwick. He pursued a career in the city, co-founding a successful business development agency, before returning to the theatre. He has worked in various capacities for Really Useful Theatre, Headlong Theatre, Out of the Blue Productions, The Onassis Programme, Iris Theatre, and The Associated Studios.

Recent producing credits include *Tosca* (OperaUpClose/ Soho Theatre), *Mary Queen of Scots Got Her Head Chopped Off* (TheatreUpClose), *Ballo* (OperaUpClose), *Quasimodo* (TheatreUpClose), *L'elisir d'amore* (OperaUpClose), *La Bohème* (OperaUpClose at Charing Cross Theatre), *Tosca*

(OperaUpClose), *Vieux Carré* (King's Head Theatre and Charing Cross Theatre), *Carmen* (OperaUpClose), *Someone To Blame* (King's Head Theatre), *La Fanciulla del West* (OperaUpClose), *Constance* (King's Head Theatre), *Manifest Destiny* (OperaUpClose), *The Turn of the Screw* (OperaUpClose), *A Cavalier For Milady* (Cock Tavern and Jermyn Street Theatre), *I Never Get Dressed Till After Dark On Sundays* (Cock Tavern), *Pagliacci* (OperaUpClose), *Madam Butterfly* (OperaUpClose), *The Barber of Seville* (OperaUpClose), *The Wind in the Willows* (Iris Theatre), *Romeo and Juliet* (Iris Theatre). Dominic is the Executive Director of OperaUpClose and the King's Head Theatre, and Board Member of Rowan Arts, an Islington-based charity acting as a catalyst for social change through the arts.

Rachel Lerman | PRODUCER

Producing credits include *Tosca* (OperaUpClose/Soho Theatre) *Mary Queen of Scots Got Her Head Chopped Off* (TheatreUpClose), *Ballo* (OperaUpClose), *Quasimodo* (TheatreUpClose), *L'elisir d'amore* (OperaUpClose), *Tosca* (OperaUpClose), *Denial* (King's Head Theatre), *La Fanciulla del West* (or West End Girl) (OperaUpClose), as Associate Producer *Don Giovanni* (OperaUpClose/Soho Theatre) and as Assistant Producer *Madam Butterfly*, *The Barber of Seville* and *Pagliacci* (all for OperaUpClose). She worked with *Belt Up Theatre* on their award-winning production of *Metamorphosis* at NSDF 2008 and *A Clockwork Orange* at the York Theatre Royal. She also writes, performs and produces for comedy group *Sad Faces*, with whom she has worked on two BBC radio programmes, *Four Sad Faces* and *Play & Record*, and five Edinburgh Fringe Festival shows, including *Sad Faces Threw A Party* (Pleasance) and *Sad Faces Remember It Differently* (Underbelly). She graduated from the University of York in 2009 with a First Class BA (Hons) in History.

Executive

Artistic Director, King's Head Theatre	Adam Spreadbury-Maher
Artistic Director, OperaUpClose	Robin Norton-Hale
Executive Director	Dominic Haddock

Production

Senior Producer	Rachel Lerman
Touring Producer	Ellie Stone
Producer	Liz Aspinall

Administrative

Theatre Manager	Louisa Davis
Development Officer	Abigail Pickard Price

King's Head Theatre Associates

Associate Director	Robin Norton-Hale
Associate Director	Robert Chevara
Associate Director	Hamish MacDougall
Associate Artist	Shelley Lang
Associate Artist	Nathan Lang
Literary Manager	Nika Obydzinski
Archivist	Carly Donaldson-Randall

OperaUpClose Associates

Associate Director	Adam Spreadbury-Maher
Associate Director	Mark Ravenhill

Artistic Patrons

Sir Jonathan Miller, Joanna Lumley OBE, Sir Tom Stoppard,
Sir Alan Parker, Janie Dee, Barry Humphries CBE

115 Upper Street | London N1 1QN
info@kingsheadtheatre.com
Tel: 0207 226 8561
@KingsHeadThtr

A BRIEF HISTORY OF
THE KING'S HEAD THEATRE BUILDING

The King's Head Theatre stands on a plot of land that has been used as a public house since 1543, though for most of its history it has been known as the King's Head Tavern (the name itself coming from an old story about Henry VIII supposedly stopping for a pint on his way to see his mistress). The current building dates back to the 1800s.

Dan Crawford took over the venue in 1970, and founded the King's Head Theatre in a room that had been used as a boxing ring and pool hall, establishing the first pub theatre in London since Shakespeare's day. Under his leadership the pub became well-known for ringing up pounds, shillings and pence until 2008, a full thirty-seven years after the rest of the UK had switched to decimal currency. Five years on, the old till still sits behind the bar. The pub is packed full of other period details, including gas lights, the original bar, old photography, and coal fires that burn continuously throughout the winter.

Crawford led the venue for thirty-five years, establishing it as a breeding ground for new talent and great work. The walls of the pub display the multitude of famous faces that began their career here. In 2010, Olivier Award-winning UpClose Productions became the theatre's resident company, and Adam Spreadbury-Maher was appointed the venue's second Artistic Director, working alongside Robin Norton-Hale who leads the company's opera programme. UpClose Productions produce at least eight shows a year, and curate the work of visiting companies all year round. The venue's reputation for nurturing new talent continues, with pioneering Trainee Director scheme (winner of the Royal Anniversary Trust Award in 1992) still being run by UpClose Productions. Recent graduates have gone on to work at the National Theatre, RSC, Lyric Hammersmith and the Globe, plus many other internationally-renowned companies.

The building is continually evolving. Recent additions to the theatre include the introduction of allocated seating and new house lights in the auditorium, with many more exciting and innovative changes planned for the future.

THEATREUPCLOSE

WOULD YOU LIKE TO BE OUR FRIEND?

If you like the work we're doing here at the King's Head Theatre, perhaps you'd like to support us by becoming a Friend or Patron of the Theatre.

We are a completely unfunded producing house and so we rely on box office sales and kind donations from members of the public who share our artistic vision and believe in what we're doing.

If you would like to join us and help us continue to produce high-quality work at affordable prices, there are a number of ways to do so:

Become a Friend   £25 per year (£40 for couples)

Receive our weekly *What's On* newsletter
Acknowledgment on our website

Key to the Stage Door   £150 per year (£200 for couples)

All the benefits of being a Friend, plus:
Invitations to patrons' events

Key to the Dressing Room   £500 per year

All the benefits of the Stage Door, plus:
Priority ticket booking
Free programmes for OperaUpClose and TheatreUpClose productions

Key to the Theatre   £1,000 per year

All the benefits of the Dressing Room, plus:
Reserved seats at any performance
Drinks with the creative team

To discuss becoming a Friend please contact Abigail Pickard Price on friends@kingsheadtheatre.com or call 020 7226 8561

Check the website www.kingsheadtheatre.com
for more information.

PATRONS AND SPONSORS

We are only able to carry on producing work of the quality we strive for through fundraising activities, our patrons and sponsors, and by selling tickets through our box office. Our Patrons and Sponsors support us with a range of valuable contributions which allow us to continue our work, acquire particular assets we need and to fund productions.

Founder Patron — Tower Leasing

Founder Sponsor — Buff Snacks

Patrons

Inger Alström, Gareth Cadwaller, David Crook, Abigail Day, Conrad Freedman, Dan Leach, Nancy Neville, Ian Simpson, John Ward, Jude Wheway and Peter Shakesby

Friends

David Allardice, Dr Angus Armstrong, Alan D. Ashmole, Jeremy Baker, Marian Bennett, Claudia Birchall, Sarah Boardman, David Brown, Chris Bulford, Diane Burridge, John Bushell, Annie Caird, Antonia Calogeras, Professor Jane Caplan, Ian Carson, Martin Collins, Christopher Cordess, Fiona Cramb, Loraine Da Costa, Cyril Dainow, Bernard & Georgina David, Owen Davies, Sheilagh Davies, Jonathan & Natalya de Lance-Holmes, Xavier De Sousa, S C Derungs, Carol Doughty, Michelle Dunn, John Farrall, Jacky Fenton, Chris Finch, Peter Fingret, Gail Fitzgerald, Marco Franchi, Jeff Gilbert, Ulrich Goser, Julia Goschalk, Rita Gromb, Kevin Gwilt, Simon Harper, Beth Herzfield, Andrew Hochhauser, Simon Holt, Joyce & Ben Hytner, Simon Jones, Jan Knight, Jonathan Levy, Susan Loppert, Fiona Lukes, Lawrence Mallison, Graham Marchant, Rosaleen McKee, David & Michelle Millington, Adrienne Morgan, Amanda Moulson, Wade Newmark, George Nissen, Irene O'Connell, Caroline Orr, Oonagh Peploe, Nigel Pleming, Mary Robertson, Dr Chris Rogers, Ivan K. Rowland, Bridget Somekh, Sir Tom Stoppard, John Tagholm, Peter Tausig, Keith Wallace, Richard Wallace-Reid, Sophie & Stephen Warshaw.

TheatreUpClose would like to thank...

John Keevill, Blerim Hysa, Sue Summers, Rosie Hytner, Alison Lurie, Almeida Theatre, Frank Penter and Shalini Simpson, Christopher Tribble, John Flower at Dr Challoner's Grammar School and the following students at East 15 Acting School: Jonathan Hopwood, Sean Bridgeman, Ryan Kirwan, Tom Coliandris, Nadia Lamin, Ella Gamble, Martin Lomas, Gerel Falconer, Duncan Mason, Natalia Hinds, Jodie McGregor, Christopher Hoen, Obi Obiora, Simon J. White, Tanawat Katatikorn, Nina Fransson, Wez Thurston, Matthew Wallbank, Phyil Webb, Jessica Smith, Hannah Elcock, Kit Fordham, Larry Akin, Hannah Ballard, Hywel Price, Lara Van Der Heijden, Emma Wilkinson, Amy Cassell, Rae Simpson, Matt Farley, Will Kenny, Aaron Agius, Beatrice Frend, Joseph Humber, Azeem Lone, Abigail Smith, John Cantlow, Nathan Bradley, Mary-Anne Hi, Jake Pike, Hannah Walker, Emma Froud, Leah Green, Marcin Rudy and Ingrid Gray.

Bloomsbury Theatre

REHEARSAL STUDIO

Attractive | modern
11m x 8m | 36ft x 26 ft
Sprung dance floor | mirrored wall | piano | kitchenette |
adjustable lighting
Shop and café on site
Easily accessible | centrally located
Available Monday-Saturday

Enquiries:
0207 679 2777
15 Gordon Street | London | WC1H 0AH
www.thebloomsbury.com

THE TERENCE RATTIGAN SOCIETY

The Terence Rattigan Society was founded in 2011, one of many events that year celebrating the centenary of the birth of the playwright widely recognised as perhaps Britain's greatest twentieth century dramatist – Terence Rattigan. The Society exists to promote, study, explore, but above all, enjoy Rattigan's work.

Terence Mervyn Rattigan (June 10th 1911 – November 30th, 1977) was born in London, the son of the troubled marriage of a British diplomat and an Edwardian beauty. His passion for the theatre was born early when, aged six, he was taken to a performance of *Cinderella*. He began writing plays while still at school and enjoyed his first success in 1933 while at Trinity College, Oxford, when a play, written with a fellow undergraduate, was produced in London. A serious comedy depicting the loose lives and loves of a group of Oxford undergraduates, *First Episode*, caused a minor scandal and in 1934 was briefly transferred to the West End. As a result John Gielgud invited him to work on an adaptation of Dickens' *A Tale of Two Cities*. But, for reasons having nothing to do with the play's merits, it was not produced. During the next two years Rattigan wrote play after play but each was rejected. Then, with his father's help, he got a job as a junior member of a team of hack screen-writers at Warner Brothers' Teddington Studios.

Rattigan's fortunes changed dramatically in November 1936. One of his rejected comedies, *French Without Tears*, about students studying at a crammer in France, was put on as a cheap stopgap at the Criterion Theatre and became an unexpected smash hit. It ran for over 1,000 performances and turned its author and young, little-known cast – including Rex Harrison, Roland Culver and Trevor Howard – into stars. This sudden change in Rattigan's fortunes triggered what he later described as a nervous breakdown. During the next six years he completed only one full length play – *After the Dance*

(1939), a powerful drama about failure, loss of ideals and unequal love. It received good reviews but, with the outbreak of World War Two, closed after just 60 performances. Advised by a psychiatrist to experience active service, Rattigan became an R.A.F. Air Gunner/Wireless Operator flying missions with Coastal Command. This experience ushered in the most successful period of his career. In just twelve years he produced ten plays, including *Flare Path* (1942), *While the Sun Shines* (1943) – which ran for over 1,000 performances – The Winslow Boy (1946), *The Browning Version* (1948), *The Deep Blue Sea* (1952) and *Separate Tables* (1954), plus screenplays for more than a dozen films, including *The Way To The Stars*, *Journey Together*, *Brighton Rock* and *The Sound Barrier*.

However, the arrival of a new, younger generation of actors and writers in the 1950s – the success of Samuel Becket's *Waiting For Godot*, the first visit to London of Bertolt Brecht's Berliner Ensemble and, above all, the opening of John Osborne's *Look Back In Anger* in May 1956 – made Rattigan and his contemporaries appear old-fashioned. This impression was heightened by Rattigan himself who wrote articles and gave ill-advised press interviews belittling the new theatrical generation and their work. Out of favour with the critics and deeply discouraged, Rattigan devoted increased amounts of time to writing highly paid film scripts – among them *The Prince and The Showgirl* (1957 starring Marilyn Monroe and Laurence Olivier), *The V.I.P.s* (1963) and *The Yellow Rolls Royce* (1964). However, during this final period of his career Rattigan also produced three of his finest plays – *Man and Boy* (1963), *In Praise of Love* (1973) and *Cause Célèbre* (1977). By his death, in 1977, Rattigan's reputation was again on the rise.

In the years since then his reputation, and the number of revivals of his work, have continued to grow. In his centenary year, 2011, there were outstanding London revivals of, among others, *Flare Path*, *Cause Célèbre*, *The Browning Version* at Chichester and, during the build-up to the centenary, a superb production of *After The Dance* at The National Theatre. The centenary also saw the "world premiere" of a 'lost' 1944 play *Less Than Kind* and a stage adaptation of his unproduced TV play Nijinsky, plus a range of exhibitions, cinema retrospectives and other Rattigan events.

Revivals continue – earlier this year a major production of *The Winslow Boy* at The Old Vic and now this production of his and Gielgud's never professionally staged *A Tale of Two Cities*. Today, widely regarded as the English Chekhov, Rattigan's plays, while firmly rooted in the times in which they were written, remain as true and emotionally engaging as at the time of their composition. Their characters remain as real and their problems as deeply moving, the plays' themes and the issues of fundamental principle and morality with which they deal as relevant, and the comedies as hilariously funny as ever.

Membership of The Terence Rattigan Society offers members a regular magazine with articles by leading playwrights, biographers and critics, theatre listings, news and views. There are theatre visits at discount prices and trips to places associated with Rattigan – his birthplace, his home at Albany, his schools, etc. plus exhibitions, masterclasses and a range of other events associated with Rattigan. But perhaps the greatest benefit of membership is the opportunity to meet like-minded people who share your enthusiasm for the work and the man.

DO JOIN US

Contact: Diana Scotney, Membership Secretary

Phone 01462-623941 | **Email** dianascotney@virginmedia.com

www.theterencerattigansociety.co.uk

Terence Rattigan met John Gielgud as an undergraduate whilst performing in the Oxford University Drama Society's 1932 production of *Romeo and Juliet*. The already-established Gielgud directed the production, with Rattigan taking on one of the smaller roles of a character who discovers Juliet's body. The undergraduates played all of the male roles and professional actresses Peggy Ashcroft and Edith Evans played the female roles, with set design by the Motley Design Group. Rattigan's performance was received by the audience with embarrassing laughter as he failed to deliver his one line correctly night after night. But out of the production came a new friendship with the increasingly celebrated Gielgud, and subsequent integration into his theatrical and homosexual circles.

In 1934 Rattigan had slight success as a playwright with *First Episode*, co-authored with Philip Heimann. *First Episode* opened at Surrey's 'Q' Theatre, where it was received warmly and transferred immediately to the Comedy Theatre in London's West End. Although the transfer was not a financial success for Rattigan, his first taste of mild artistic success was enough for him to drop out of Oxford and move to London to commence a full time career as a playwright.

It was Gielgud's boyfriend John Perry who suggested he approach Rattigan as a potential collaborator for *A Tale of Two Cities*. Gielgud, having recently finished a highly successful tour of *Hamlet*, desired to play both the hero Sydney Carton and antagonist Marquis de St Evrémonde. In essence, Gielgud sought someone to write the dialogue for the adaptation whilst he would be responsible for the play's construction, taking a largely dramaturgical role.

Gielgud, following Perry's guidance, spoke to Rattigan. "I can't find anyone to do this *Tale of Two Cities*. You're not doing anything – I'm sure you're not doing anything. Would you like to do it?" Gielgud walked away, returning quickly to add, "I wonder if it's alright to have anyone without any experience?"

Whilst Gielgud's offer would have an undeniable impact on Rattigan's career, he was not primarily concerned with advancing Rattigan from his station of a one-time West End playwright of only moderate success. By comparison, at this time, Gielgud was a celebrated and sought-after theatrical star, his self-directed performances in *Richard II* and *Hamlet* having received global acclaim.

In the spring of 1935 the two began work together at Gielgud's home in Finchingfield, with Rattigan quickly writing the dialogue under his collaborator's supervision. Gielgud dictated the order and location of the scenes, keen for the adaptation to focus on the domestic relationships of the Manettes, Defarges and St Evrémondes, whilst avoiding exploration of the historical revolutionary settings in great detail. There is no storming of the Bastille; instead, the historical context of the novel and period are exposed through Rattigan's finessed yet straightforward dialogue.

Once the prologue and first two acts were completed, Gielgud took the draft to Bronson Albery, for whom he was currently appearing in *Noah* at the New Theatre in the West End. Bronson was keen to impress Gielgud, and they had been working together for sometime by this point. Bronson's response was extremely positive, promising to produce *A Tale of Two Cities* at one of his West End theatres that autumn, provided that the final act matched the quality of the material already written. A mere three weeks later, the third act was completed and submitted, after which it took only a fortnight for the suitably impressed Albery to programme a production for autumn 1935. Gielgud would get to play Sydney Carton and, perhaps more significantly, Rattigan's career as a West End playwright was set to be secured with his second production.

The Motley Design Group, who had worked on the 1932 OUDS production of *Romeo and Juliet*, were brought onto the project to design a breathtaking set for *A Tale of Two Cities* at the New Theatre and a cast was assembled, including Fay Compton as Lucie Manette and Martitia Hunt as Miss Pross.

Just before rehearsals were ready to commence, enter Sir John Martin-Harvey.

Martin-Harvey was a leading actor-manager of the day, who had been playing Sydney Carton in *The Only Way*, his own adaptation of *A Tale of Two Cities*, since 1899. His adaptation was also a successful 1927 black and white silent film, starring Martin-Harvey alongside Madge Stuart and Betty Faire.

Gielgud received what he described as an "emotionally violent" letter from the 72-year-old Martin-Harvey, begging him to delay the premiere of his new adaptation until he had finished his own farewell tours of *The Only Way*. Gielgud took the letter to Bronson, who subsequently asked his fraternity of fellow theatre owners and critics at the Garrick Club for advice. To Gielgud's reported surprise, Bronson agreed with Martin-Harvey and the production was aborted. Gielgud set to work immediately devising an alternative production for the dates he had secured at the New Theatre, leading to a production of *Romeo and Juliet* in which himself and Lawrence Olivier alternated in the roles of Romeo and Mercutio, whilst Peggy Ashcroft and Edith Evans reprised their roles from Gielgud's previous production at Oxford.

Gielgud broke the news to Rattigan with trademark nonchalance. "It's a pity about Martin-Harvey, isn't it? But it's lucky the design works for *Romeo and Juliet*, so we can do that instead. Larry says he'll do Mercutio. Isn't it marvellous?" It is reported that, upon returning to his room, Rattigan wept.

The Motley's set, designed and built for the now defunct *A Tale of Two Cities*, was modified only slightly for *Romeo and Juliet*. Photographs of the production are available in several publications and within the theatre collection of the Victoria and Albert museum in London. The images provide a powerful insight into what was surely a traumatic experience for Rattigan when he inevitably attended the premiere of Gielgud and Olivier's production, forced to watch a set and an actor originally intended for his own play.

Rattigan proceeded, of course, to become one of the most significant playwrights of the twentieth-century, with his seminal plays *French Without Tears*, *After the Dance*, *Flare Path*, *The Winslow Boy*, *The Browning Version*, and *The Deep Blue Sea* being just a few of his impressive oeuvre.

Perhaps because of the cruelty with which his *Tale* was cancelled, and the subsequent explosive success of his own original material, Rattigan paid no more attention to the collaboration with Gielgud in his lifetime. It was Rattigan's style to bury projects he deemed to be commercially and artistically unsuccessful, as he did with *After The Dance*, which, despite opening to ecstatic reviews, closed under the dark clouds of the Second World War.

Despite Rattigan's attempt to bury the piece, which included no publications, sparse references in literature and no professional productions, his *A Tale of Two Cities* has surfaced three times between its creation in 1935 and professional world stage premiere in 2013 at the King's Head Theatre in London. In 1950 schoolboys at St Brendon's College, Clifton, performed the play. A 70-minute radio adaptation was broadcast by the BBC in 1950, which starred Eric Portman as Sydney Carton and received favourable rather than overwhelming reviews. Lastly, in February 2013, a production was staged at the East 15 drama school in London, performed by their third year acting students.

I first discovered the existence of the play in 2011 during Rattigan's centenary celebrations, whilst London was awash with brilliant Rattigan revivals and the world premiere of *Less Than Kind*. In the summer, whilst working at The Cock Tavern in Kilburn, I began my search for a piece for the theatre to produce as part of the 100th birthday party making its way across London. The only parameter to be met, a result of my own imposed artistic policy, was that selected piece had to be new. *A Tale of Two Cities* was vaguely referenced on Wikipedia, in Rattigan's two biographies and the introduction to his collected works. Excited and intrigued, I contacted the Rattigan estate for a copy of the script. After reading it I requested a licence for performance for 2011, but the play had already been optioned by another much larger and richer (subsidised) theatre, scheduled for production during Charles Dickens' 2012 bicentenary. In this David and Goliath battle, I lost. For the time being.

I remained in contact with the wonderful Sarah McNair at Alan Brodie for the following 18 months, and suggested a staging with a London drama school to see the script in performance. Phil Weaver at East 15 showed immediate interest at the prospect of his students working on the project, and so a second amateur production was staged in the Corbett Theatre with a group of 14 talented and enthusiastic actors on the eve of their graduation. Stewart Agnew played Sydney Carton, the role originally intended for Gielgud, and will be making his professional debut as Carton in the King's Head Theatre production, for which I am writing these notes. The six-week rehearsal process at East 15 offered the time needed to unstitch the process by which Rattigan and Gielgud adapted Dickens' novel in amazing speed in 1935, resulting in an invaluable, intimate knowledge of the adaptation.

Immediately after the successful production at East 15 the editing process began, which would ultimately take the script from three and a half hours and 40 actors down to two and a half hours and eight actors. Following the work at East 15, the script went through months of further cuts and adaptations, plus several readings with many generous actors, before being submitted to Rattigan's representation. At last, the script has reached publication. You have it in your hands now and, I hope, are watching a production or planning to produce this beautiful play somewhere in the world.

It was so important to me that what I helped in delivering to the world for the first time in print and on stage is an adaptation of which both the estates of Rattigan and Gielgud can be immensely proud, a script that was completely true to the work of Dickens, Rattigan and Gielgud, but also was a play for today, both in terms of its artistic merits and style, coupled with the economic austerity we currently live in.

A Tale of Two Cities is the world's most successful novel, having sold over 200 million copies. There are eight film adaptations and five for television. And now, for the very first time, here is a new stage adaptation. This adaptation marries for the first and only time Sirs Terence Rattigan and John Gielgud, alongside the master novelist Charles Dickens. It has been my proud honour and privilege to have been involved with this script and project for several years, and I hope you enjoy it as much as I have.

Adam Spreadbury-Maher
Editor & Director
A Tale of Two Cities
September 2013

This play is for a cast of eight actors:

1. SYDNEY CARTON
Also COACHMAN and MARQUIS DE ST EVREMONDE.

2. JARVIS LORRY
Also JUDGE and ROAD-MENDER.

3. CHARLES DARNAY
Also GUARD and ERNEST DEFARGE.

4. MADME DEFARGE
Also PASSENGER 2, RUNNER, EDWARD STRYVER, CLERK
and GUARD 2.

5. LUCIE MANETTE
Also PASSENGER 1, CHILD and FRANCOIS.

6. MISS PROSS
Also SOLICITOR-GENERAL, GABELLE, WOMAN and
SEAMSTRESS.

7. DOCTOR MANETTE
Also GASPARD.

8. JERRY CRUNCHER
Also JOHN BASARD, MAN and GUARD 1.

PROLOGUE

The Dover road, November, 1785. Night.

The stage is pitch black; faces can only be seen by handheld lanterns. Three passengers walk beside a coach without lanterns; the COACHMAN and GUARD carry lanterns, the GUARD walking behind with a blunderbuss. The COACHMAN is encouraging the horses.

COACHMAN

Not much further, gentlemen. We're nearly on top of Shooter's now. Joe, can you hear anything?

GUARD

(Listening) Sounds like a horse at a canter.

COACHMAN

At the gallop, Joe. At the gallop and coming this way. Listen!

GUARD

You're right. *(Jumping onto his perch and seizing his blunderbuss)* Inside, ladies and gentlemen.

PASSENGER 1

(Hesitating) Do you think—could it be a highwayman?

GUARD

It could.

PASSENGER 2

Oh no. Oh dear! What shall I do? I haven't a pistol.

LORRY
Is your blunderbuss loaded?

GUARD
Never mind about my blunderbuss. Get in the coach, sir.

LORRY
But I have nothing for him to take.

GUARD
Only your life.

    The PASSENGERS *get into the coach.*

(Shouting) Hi there! Stand or I fire.

A VOICE
Is that the Dover Mail?

GUARD
Who are you?

VOICE
I want a passenger.

GUARD
Which passenger?

VOICE
Mr Jarvis Lorry.

GUARD
What's your business with Mr Jarvis Lorry?

VOICE
I've a message for him.

    One of the passengers sticks his head through the window.

LORRY
My name is Jarvis Lorry.

GUARD

Very well, sir. You'd better get out. *(Shouting)* Mr Lorry is here. You can come on slowly. But remember, I've got a blunderbuss here and it's aiming at your head.

LORRY

What's the matter? Who is it? Is it Jerry?

JERRY

(Appearing) Yes, Mr Lorry, it's me. *(To* GUARD*)* All right, you. You can put that blunderbuss of yours away. Mr Lorry knows me. I'm no ruddy highwayman.

LORRY

Yes, yes, guard. That's right. His name is Jerry Cruncher. He's a messenger at Tellson's Bank in London, where I work myself. Well, Jerry, what is it?

> *The two men are given a degree of privacy.*

JERRY

I've a message from the bank, sir. They told me to say *(Reciting)* you are to meet the young lady at the George Inn at Dover. She will be accompanied by her governess, a Miss Pross. Passages have been reserved for you on the night packet to Calais.

LORRY

(Impatiently) Yes, yes, I know all that. What else?

JERRY

(Conspiratorially) The place you've to go to is *(Reading from a piece of paper)* Defarge's Wine Shop, Place of St Antoine, Paris.

> LORRY *takes the paper, repeats the address, then gives* JERRY *a coin.*

LORRY

Thank you, Jerry. Here's half a crown for a drink.

JERRY

Thank you, Mr Lorry. Shall I give any answer?

LORRY

Answer? Yes. Three words, Jerry. Don't forget—just say: "Recalled to life".

He gets into the coach.

JERRY

Recalled to life? *(To* GUARD*)* Now, ain't that a blasted queer answer?

GUARD

Blasted queer. *(To* COACHMAN*)* All right, Tom. Whip 'em up.

The COACHMAN *shouts to the horses.*

End of scene.

ACT ONE

SCENE ONE

The place of St Antoine, Paris. Defarge's Wine Shop.

MADAME DEFARGE *is knitting behind the counter, when* LUCIE, MISS PROSS *and* LORRY *enter.* LORRY *looks round timidly.*

LORRY

(To MADAME DEFARGE*)* Good day, Madame. Is this the wine shop of Monsieur Defarge?

MADAME DEFARGE *nods.*

Where may I find Monsieur Defarge? I have some business to discuss with him of a rather confidential nature.

MADAME DEFARGE *points to the bench, where they sit down.*

(To LUCIE*)* Not a very talkative lady.

LUCIE

(To MADAME DEFARGE*)* I see you had an accident with a cask, Madame.

MADAME DEFARGE *raises her head and then continues her knitting, never once looking up.*

LORRY

I trust your husband will not be long, Madame.

MADAME DEFARGE *shrugs her shoulders.*

MISS PROSS

What's the matter with you, miss? Have you lost your tongue?

    MADAME DEFARGE *pays no attention.*

Surly baggage. No manners, the French. *(She sits down with* LUCIE *and* LORRY*.)* Look at her, I ask you. Would you like to run into that on a dark night if you had half-a-crown in your purse?

LUCIE

Sh, Prossie.

MISS PROSS

(Glares at MADAME DEFARGE*)* Ugh! I hate the French. The sooner we're out of this country and back on English soil the better for all of us.

LORRY

That may be tomorrow, if all goes well.

LUCIE

Then you really believe my father is here?

LORRY

The wine shop of Monsieur Defarge, at St Antoine's, Paris. That was my message. There can be no mistake about it.

LUCIE

It doesn't seem possible.

MISS PROSS

(With a sniff) Your father's dead, child. Has been for nearly twenty years, as I very well know.

LORRY

My dear Miss Pross, you don't seem quite to realise what the Bastille is.

MISS PROSS

It's a prison, isn't it? Only French.

LORRY

Yes, it's a prison.

MISS PROSS

Then if Dr Manette was there for twenty years he must have done something very wicked, and I for one don't believe it.

LORRY

(Impressively) We are in France, Miss Pross. Men can be thrown into the Bastille prison and rot there for the rest of their lives, and the only offence they committed might be a rash word against the King, or a slight to some great noble.

MISS PROSS

Anything's possible in France, I admit. But you'll never get me to believe your story, for all that. Dr Manette is dead.

LUCIE

(Restrainingly) Prossie.

LORRY

(Simultaneously) I did not invent this story. I only know what I have been told by the manager of Tellson's Bank himself, that Lucie's father did not die twenty years ago, as we all imagined, but was imprisoned in the Bastille. He has only lately been released, and he is being sheltered here by a man called Defarge. That is all I have been told.

> MISS PROSS *is growing impatient.* DEFARGE *appears at the door.*

LORRY

Monsieur Defarge, I believe?

DEFARGE

Yes.

LORRY

I've some business I'd like to discuss with you. *(In a low voice)* It concerns someone who has been recalled to life.

MADAME DEFARGE *looks up quickly.*

DEFARGE
(Sharply) Ah. You're from Tellson's?

LORRY
Yes.

DEFARGE
(Glaring at LUCIE*)* And the lady?

LORRY
His daughter.

DEFARGE
Does she know?

LORRY
Yes.

DEFARGE
I'm happy to meet you, mademoiselle.

LUCIE
(Eagerly) Monsieur Defarge. My father—is he here?

DEFARGE
Yes, mademoiselle.

LUCIE
He is alive and well?

DEFARGE
He is alive, mademoiselle. *(To* LORRY*)* Did may people see you
come here? You should have come at night.

LUCIE
Why? Is my father still in danger?

DEFARGE
I am in danger, mademoiselle, for sheltering him.

LUCIE

It is kind of you, monsieur.

DEFARGE

A long time ago I was his servant. He was good to me. I am glad to help him now.

MADAME DEFARGE *brings over a key.*

DEFARGE

This is my wife.

LORRY

We have already had some conversation with Madame Defarge.

MADAME DEFARGE *returns to her seat.*

LORRY

Well now, Miss Pross, I think perhaps you had best wait here while we go with monsieur.

MISS PROSS

With her for company? *(She jerks a thumb at* MADAME DEFARGE.*)* I'm going to have a gay time.

MISS PROSS *sits down as* DEFARGE *ushers* LUCIE *and* LORRY *into a passage where a staircase leads up to the attic.*

DEFARGE

Shall we go up?

LUCIE *and* LORRY *move slowly towards the stairs.*

I'll lead the way.

He begins to climb the staircase. LORRY *supports* LUCIE *up the stairs.* DEFARGE *reaches the top and opens a door. A knocking can be heard.*

LUCIE

What is that knocking?

DEFARGE

Come along, mademoiselle, and be careful.

LUCIE *climbs the rest of the stairs, supported by* LORRY. *The knocking becomes louder.*

The room to which they are being led is seen. DR MANETTE *sits stooping over a cobbler's last and hammering at a pair of shoes.* DEFARGE *enters but* DR MANETTE *takes no notice.* DEFARGE *beckons to the other two and they come in.*

DEFARGE

(Loudly) Good day.

DR MANETTE

(Raising his head for a second, faintly) Good day.

DEFARGE

Still hard at work, I see.

DR MANETTE

Yes.

> *Pause. He continues to work.*

DEFARGE

Do you mind if I let in a little more light? Could you bear it?

DR MANETTE

What did you say?

DEFARGE

Could you bear a little more light? *(Pulls back a curtain)* Do you mean to finish that pair of shoes today?

DR MANETTE

I can't say that I mean to. I suppose so. I don't know.

> LORRY *comes forward to* DR MANETTE'S *side.* DR MANETTE *looks up, puzzled, then resumes his work.*

DEFARGE

This gentleman has come to visit you.

> DR MANETTE *looks up at* LORRY *again.*

He's come to see your work. He knows all about shoe-making. Show him the shoe you're working at now. *(To* LORRY, *in an undertone)* Take it, monsieur.

> DEFARGE *takes the shoe and hands it to* LORRY.

Tell the gentlemen what kind of shoe it is, and who made it.

DR MANETTE

(After a pause) I forget what it is you asked me. What did you say?

DEFARGE

The gentleman would like to know what kind of shoe that is.

DR MANETTE

It's a lady's shoe—a young lady's walking shoe. I made it from a pattern.

DEFARGE

And now tell him who made it.

DR MANETTE

Did you ask for my name?

DEFARGE

Yes.

DR MANETTE

One hundred and five, North Tower.

DEFARGE

Is that all?

DR MANETTE

One hundred and five, North Tower.

> DEFARGE *shrugs his shoulders and steps back.*

LORRY

You are not a shoe-maker by trade?

DR MANETTE

No. I—I learnt it here. I asked leave to teach myself, and after a long time they gave it me. So I have made shoes ever since.

LORRY

Dr Manette, do you remember nothing of me? In Paris, twenty years ago, don't you remember? And this man. *(Holding* DEFARGE'S *arm)* Don't you remember? He was your servant.

DR MANETTE

(After a pause) Do you like that shoe? May I have it back?

LORRY

(Handing it back) Yes, yes, it is very well made.

> DR MANETTE *takes it and resumes his work on it.* LORRY *steps back.*

DEFARGE

(To LORRY*)* Can you recognise him?

LORRY

I couldn't have believed it possible. It's—it's appalling.

DEFARGE

I suppose it is—to an Englishman. We Frenchmen find it hard to be appalled these days.

> LUCIE *steps forward quietly to her father's side. He continues to work until his eyes catch her dress, then he looks up, a shoe-maker's knife in his hand.* LORRY *and* DEFARGE *start forward, but she quietly motions them back.*

DR MANETTE

Who are you?

> LUCIE *makes no reply.*

You don't work here, do you?

> LUCIE *shakes her head.*

Who are you?

LUCIE *sits beside him. He recoils from her. She lays her head on his shoulder. He looks at her, puzzled.*

Was it you? *(He touches her hair.)* Was it you?

She makes no reply.

I think she laid her head on my shoulders that night when they came to take me away. I didn't know they would take me to the North Tower. It was you, wasn't it?

He points the knife at her, with no intention of violence. LORRY *and* DEFARGE *step forward.*

LUCIE

Stay where you are, please, and don't speak.

DR MANETTE

Whose voice was that? It was hers, I think. I wish I could remember. *(After a pause)* Who are you? What IS your name?

LUCIE

One day I'll tell you my name. Not now, not now.

After a pause DR MANETTE *goes to return to his work.* LUCIE *gently takes the knife out of his hand.*

DR MANETTE

May I have that, please? I need it for my work.

LUCIE

You don't have to work any more, now. You're coming away with me to a place where you won't have to make shoes any more.

DR MANETTE

Am I to leave the North Tower?

LUCIE

(To LORRY *and* DEFARGE*)* We must take him away at once.

LORRY

But is he fit for the journey?

DEFARGE

Mademoiselle is right. The sooner he is out of this country, the better for him.

LORRY

I'll go now and hire a carriage and post-horses. *(To* LUCIE*)* We'd better go at once. Come, my dear.

LUCIE

I must stay with him.

LORRY

You're not afraid to be here alone?

LUCIE

Afraid—with him?

DR MANETTE

Why am I to leave the North Tower?

LUCIE

Because you're free now.

DR MANETTE

Free?

LUCIE

You're going on a long journey with me to a country where you'll forget about the North Tower, and where you'll be very, very happy. Oh god, may that be true.

DR MANETTE

Am I to go with you?

LUCIE

Yes, you're to go with me. Oh, I hope you care to go with me. I hope you care to be recalled to life.

DR MANETTE
I can't say.

> DEFARGE *motions* LORRY *to the door, and they go out.*
>
> *End of scene.*

SCENE TWO

Calais-Dover packet. Only a small part of the deck is seen.

LUCIE, DR MANETTE and MISS PROSS *are sitting, swathed in travelling rugs.* MISS PROSS *is holding a handkerchief to her mouth and* DR MANETTE *is asleep. A* MAN *standing in the background looks over the rails.*

LORRY *appears.*

LORRY

The tide is favourable, the captain says. We are putting into harbour now.

MISS PROSS

Thank God.

LORRY

(To LUCIE*)* How is he?

LUCIE

Still asleep.

LORRY

We must wake him, I'm afraid. We shall be alongside in a very few minutes.

LUCIE

Must we wake him? He is so peaceful now. The noise and the crowds will frighten him again, as they did at Calais.

LORRY

My dear, there is no choice. We cannot carry him ashore.

MISS PROSS

If anyone is to be carried ashore it will have to be me.

LORRY

(Insincerely) My poor Miss Pross, I feel for you.

MISS PROSS

Thank you. I can feel for myself.

LORRY

(To LUCIE*)* I shall go and collect our luggage. Will you wait here for me?

> The MAN *looking over the rails turns and comes forward.*

MAN

You must pardon me, Madam, but I could not help overhearing your conversation just now. I gather your father is not well.

LUCIE

Sir, he is very ill.

> *She goes to wake* DR MANETTE, *but the* MAN *restrains her.*

MAN

No. Let him sleep. When we are alongside, I shall try, with your permission, to carry him ashore without waking him.

LUCIE

It is very kind—

MAN

No, no. I shall be most glad to help you.

MISS PROSS

And who, sir, might you be?

MAN

Charles Darnay, madam, of Berkeley Square, London, and your most obedient servant.

MISS PROSS

Well, Mr Charles Darnay of Berkeley Square, London, are you usually in the habit of accosting strange ladies aboard packet boats?

DARNAY

Truthfully, madam, I am not.

MISS PROSS

(With dignity) Then I must ask you, sir—*(She puts her handkerchief to her mouth and looks round urgently.)* Where is the ladies' saloon?

DARNAY

(Sympathetically) Down the steps and on your right.

>   MISS PROSS *disappears quickly.* LUCIE *smiles at* DARNAY.

LUCIE

You must forgive her, Mr Darnay. She is my companion and has been with me all my life. Perhaps I allow her too much liberty.

DARNAY

On the contrary, she was entirely right. I might be the most unscrupulous rogue, for all you know.

LUCIE

I am most grateful to you, sir, indeed I am.

DARNAY

You are journeying to London?

LUCIE

We are taking the coach tonight.

DARNAY

I am taking the night coach also.

LUCIE

My name is Manette.

DARNAY

You are French?

LUCIE

I was born in France, but I have lived all my life in England. I prefer
to think of myself as English.

DARNAY

(After a pause, gloomily) I am a Frenchman, Miss Manette. I am an
exile from my country too, like you. Like you I prefer to call myself
English. But not for ever. Tyranny cannot last for ever. One day the
forces of reason, justice and liberty will prevail, and then, if I am
still alive, I shall be proud to call myself a Frenchman again.

> *There is a pause, broken by a sudden clattering and a confused
> babble of voices.*

DARNAY

We are coming alongside. *(He goes to the rail and looks over.)* He
is a fine helmsman, our captain. We always arrive punctually at
Dover.

LUCIE

You make this journey often then?

DARNAY

I have to, yes.

LUCIE

Why, since you say you are an exile from France?

DARNAY

I must beg you not to ask me that. It is a matter of business—of a
rather private sort.

> LORRY *comes back.*

LORRY

Ah, there you are, my dear. Why haven't you wakened your father?

LUCIE

This gentleman has very generously offered to carry my father ashore.

LORRY

That is very kind of you, sir. Where is Miss Pross?

LUCIE

Er—she went below. I think—

    MISS PROSS *appears.*

LORRY

(Heartily) Ah, there we are. How do we feel now?

MISS PROSS

(Glaring at him) We still feel exceedingly sick.

LORRY

Dear me—well, we shall soon be on dry land. *(He looks over the rail.)* Who are these men coming on board?

DARNAY

They look like press gangers—or Bow Street runners.

LORRY

That's what they are. Bow Street runners. We must have a criminal on board.

MISS PROSS

(Glaring at DARNAY*)* That wouldn't surprise me at all.

    DARNAY *laughs.*

LORRY

Well now, sir, if you wouldn't mind waiting here with us, until the other passengers have gone on shore, I think—

A MAN, *followed by* ANOTHER MAN, *shoulders* LORRY *aside and goes up to* DARNAY.

MAN
Are you Charles Darnay?

DARNAY
Yes.

MAN
(To the OTHER MAN*)* Take him on shore.

The MAN *grips* DARNAY'S *hands.*

MISS PROSS
Solomon.

MISS PROSS *recognises her brother and exits.*

DARNAY
What is the meaning of this? Who are you?

MAN
My name is John Barsad, at your service.

He makes a sign to the RUNNER.

RUNNER
Charles Darnay, I arrest you in the King's name on a charge of 'Igh Treason.

DARNAY
But this is fantastic. High Treason? But what have I done?

BARSAD
You'll know soon enough. *(To* LORRY*)* Here you—you were talking to this man—what do you know about him?

LORRY
Nothing, sir, I am Mr Jarvis Lorry, of Tellson's Bank in Fleet Street, London.

BARSAD

(Writing) Did you see him come on board at Calais?

LORRY

Let me see now—yes, I believe I did.

BARSAD

That'll do. You'll have to give evidence when his trial comes on. All right, you. Take him away.

> LUCIE *runs forward.*

LUCIE

Officer—

BARSAD

I'm not an officer, lady. Just a plain citizen, doing his duty to his King by informing against a dangerous spy.

LUCIE

But he's not a spy. I'm sure he's not. We have just been talking—

BARSAD

Oh. You've been talking, have you? Well—you'll have to give evidence too. *(To* LUCIE *and* LORRY*)* You'll be hearing from me, both of you. *(To the* RUNNER*)* All right.

> *He is leading him away, when* DARNAY *stops him.*

DARNAY

You are making a terrible mistake, Mr Barsad.

BARSAD

I don't think so, Mr Darnay. Anyway, I'll take the risk.

DARNAY

Very well. May I ask you a favour? I have made a promise I should like to keep.

BARSAD

What promise is that?

DARNAY

To carry this lady's father ashore. He is an invalid.

BARSAD

(After a pause) All right. But don't try any tricks. It wouldn't be healthy.

> *The* RUNNER *releases* DARNAY, *who goes to* DR MANETTE'S *chair, and gently picks him up.*

LUCIE

Mr Darnay, I—*(She hesitates)* I believe you are innocent.

DARNAY

Thank you. Good-bye.

> *Followed by* BARSAD *and the* RUNNER, DARNAY *carries* DR MANETTE *to the gang-plank.*
>
> *End of scene.*

Scene Three

The Old Bailey, London. Six months later.

On one side of the stage is the anteroom; on the other side is the courtroom. In the courtroom are barristers, the JUDGE, DARNAY *in the dock, and counsel for both sides. The* SOLICITOR-GENERAL *is addressing the jury, which is the audience. In the anteroom there is much coming and going, with barristers walking up and down and late spectators entering the courtroom.* JERRY *is at the doors*

LUCIE *and* DR MANETTE *enter the anteroom.* SYDNEY CARTON *comes in, takes his wig out of his pocket, puts it on, and goes to the doors.*

CARTON

(To JERRY*)* Is the old man still on his feet? I needn't have hurried.

He goes into court, puts his feet on the bench in front of him, and composes himself for sleep.

DR MANETTE

(To JERRY*)* Who was that?

JERRY

Mr Sydney Carton, sir. He's for the prisoner.

DR MANETTE

He's surely not leading for the defence?

JERRY

Oh no, sir. He's not leading. Mr Stryver's leading. He's only a junior is Mr Carton. *(Chuckling)* That suits him better. He can spend more time in the Hoop and Toy then.

> *The action moves to the courtroom.*

SOLICITOR-GEN

In November of last year, as he arrived at Dover by the packet, the prisoner was arrested and charged with High Treason. The evidence will show that the prisoner was in the habit of travelling in mysterious fashion between England and France, that he had many such lists of British forces as those found in his possession, and that he frequently showed these lists to Frenchmen at Calais and other French towns. Finally, I shall call several witnesses, who will state that they have personally heard the prisoner using language of a treasonable nature. But perhaps the most damning evidence will come from the prisoner's own mouth. On his own admission he is a Frenchman by birth—a Frenchman masquerading under an English name and enjoying the rights and privileges of an English subject. He may give reasons, plausible no doubt, why he should act in this manner. I think you will say, as I say, that this man has deliberately chosen to mask his real nationality behind an English name, in order to further his own nefarious ends. If you find that the prisoner is proved to have followed the loathsome, evil and traitorous occupation of a spy, you must, as twelve loyal and patriotic subjects of His Majesty King George the Third, record a vote of guilty, thus ridding the world of a most pernicious and dastardly rogue.

> *He sits down. A loud murmur breaks out in the court. The* JUDGE *blows his nose loudly,* STRYVER, *the prisoner's counsel, bends forward to say something to* SYDNEY CARTON. *The latter nods carelessly, without turning round.* STRYVER *gets to his feet.*

STRYVER

My Lord—

THE JUDGE

(Surprised) Yes, Mr Stryver?

STRYVER

I must beg your permission to retire from the court for a short while. I am not feeling well.

JUDGE

I hope it is nothing serious, Mr Stryver.

STRYVER

No, My Lord. A mere feeling of faintness. My learned friend, Mr Carton, will conduct the case of the defence in my absence.

JUDGE

Very well. I trust your attack of faintness is not in any way due to the Solicitor General's eloquence.

He enjoys his joke.

STRYVER

I find that hard to believe, My Lord.

STRYVER *goes into the anteroom. He sits down and whispers to* JERRY, *who goes out, and returns later with wine, which* STRYVER *drinks.*

JUDGE

We will proceed.

The SOLICITOR-GENERAL *rises.*

SOLICITOR-GEN

I call John Barsad.

BARSAD *goes into the witness box and takes the oath.*

Is your name John Barsad?

BARSAD

Yes.

SOLICITOR-GEN

What is your profession?

BARSAD
Gentleman.

SOLICITOR-GEN
Of private means?

BARSAD
Yes, that's right.

SOLICITOR-GEN
On the night of the third of November 1785, did you have occasion to enter the Blue Boar Tavern in Cheapside?

BARSAD
I did.

SOLICITOR-GEN
Whom did you see there?

BARSAD
The prisoner.

SOLICITOR-GEN
Was he alone?

BARSAD
No. He was with three officers.

SOLICITOR-GEN
How would you describe the prisoner's manner?

BARSAD
Highly suspicious.

SOLICITOR-GEN
In October of last year did you see the prisoner at a hotel in Dover?

BARSAD
Yes.

SOLICITOR-GEN
Did you search the prisoner's room?

BARSAD
I did.

SOLICITOR-GEN
What did you find?

BARSAD
I found three lists of forces.

SOLICITOR-GEN
(Handing him three papers) Were these the lists you found?

BARSAD
(Examining them) Yes.

> *The lists are handed to the* JURY.

SOLICITOR-GEN
Thank you, Mr Barsad.

> *He sits down.* BARSAD *prepares to leave the box.* CARTON
> *rises.*

CARTON
One moment, Mr Barsad.

> CARTON *turns to face* BARSAD.

CARTON
You say that you saw the prisoner in the Blue Boar Tavern on a
certain night in November 1785?

BARSAD
Yes, that's right.

CARTON
Mr Barsad, will you, for a moment, conquer your natural repugnance
and look straight at me?

BARSAD *looks at him.*

My Lord, I beg leave to take off my wig.

JUDGE

Is it necessary, Mr Carton, to undress yourself in order to cross-examine the witness?

CARTON

I assure you, My Lord, my wig is all I shall take off.

JUDGE

Indeed I trust so.

CARTON *takes off his wig.*

CARTON

Now, Mr Barsad, look at me closely. Do you say that you are still certain that it was the prisoner you saw in the tavern on that day?

BARSAD

(Uncertainly) Yes.

CARTON

Mr Barsad, if I told you that it was me you saw, what would your answer be?

BARSAD

I—I—Was it you?

CARTON

You're not here to ask me questions. I am asking you what your answer would be if I told you it was me you saw in that tavern on that day.

BARSAD

I don't know. You're like him.

CARTON

That is not the point, Mr Barsad. A moment ago you were saying that you were sure it was the prisoner you saw. Now you say that it might have been myself. Isn't that correct?

BARSAD

It was dark in there. I thought it was him.

CARTON

It was dark. You thought. Really, Mr Barsad, this is very different to what you have already told the jury on oath. What's the truth, Mr Barsad? Isn't it that you have no idea whom you saw in the tavern on that day?

BARSAD

I tell you I thought it was him. But you're so blasted like him.

JUDGE

(Sharply) There is no call for profanity. Mr Carton, I must confess that this is the most extraordinary manner of cross-examining a witness that I have ever heard. Am I to assume that we are now to try you for High Treason in the place of the prisoner?

CARTON

I hardly think that will be necessary, My Lord. My object was merely to discredit the witness' testimony. He at first positively identified the prisoner as the man he saw in that tavern. Now he says it could have been myself. Well, My Lord, if it could have been myself, it could easily have been anyone in England even, shall we say, Your Lordship.

JUDGE

We shall not say. You are impertinent, Mr Carton. I am not in the habit of frequenting pot-houses. Kindly dress yourself, and continue the cross-examination in a more seemly manner.

CARTON

As Your Lordship pleases. *(Resuming his wig)* Now, Mr Barsad, you have told the jury that you are a gentleman by profession?

BARSAD

Yes.

CARTON

Isn't that a rather curious profession? How long have you followed it?

BARSAD
All my life, of course.

CARTON
Does it pay well?

BARSAD
I don't understand you.

CARTON
What do you live on?

BARSAD
My—my property.

CARTON
Oh. What is your property?

BARSAD
That's no business of anyone's.

CARTON
Did you inherit it?

BARSAD
Yes.

CARTON
From whom?

BARSAD
A distant relative.

CARTON
Very distant?

BARSAD
Fairly distant.

CARTON

I see. Somewhere about the middle distance. Tell me, Mr Barsad, have you ever been in the Fleet?

BARSAD

No.

CARTON

I'm not asking you if you've ever been in the Royal Navy. I'm asking you if you've ever been in the Fleet prison for debtors.

BARSAD

What's that got to do with it?

CARTON

Come along, Mr Barsad. Have you ever been in prison for debt?

BARSAD

Oh, all right. Yes, I have.

CARTON

How many times?

BARSAD

I don't know.

CARTON

Shall we say, from time to time?

BARSAD

About three times.

CARTON

Very well. *(Quietly)* Mr Barsad, will you tell the jury how you came to be an Old Bailey spy?

SOLICITOR-GEN

I protest most strongly, My Lord, against this foul slur on my witness' honour.

JUDGE

Mr Carton, only a few moments ago I asked you to—

CARTON

I apologise, My Lord. I have always suffered from a short memory. Mr Barsad, let me put the question in this way. How much money do you expect to make out of your evidence?

BARSAD

Nothing at all.

CARTON

Your motives are solely patriotic?

BARSAD

Yes.

CARTON

You love your country dearly?

BARSAD

Yes.

CARTON

So dearly perhaps, that you're prepared to perjure yourself on her behalf. I suggest that the whole of your evidence is a tissue of lies designed to bring an innocent man to the gallows.

BARSAD

No, that's not true.

CARTON

I suggest that you never found those lists in the prisoner's room.

BARSAD

I did.

CARTON

I suggest that you compiled those lists yourself and that you have sold your false information to the government.

BARSAD
No.

CARTON
Very well, Mr Barsad. Thank you.

> BARSAD *steps down.* CARTON *sits.*

JUDGE
(As if to himself) I hope Mr Stryver is feeling better.

SOLICITOR-GEN
I call Miss Lucie Manette.

> LUCIE *comes into the courtroom and goes into the box.*

Is your name Lucie Manette?

> LUCIE *is looking at the prisoner. Their eyes meet and she smiles at him.*

Please. Is your name Lucie Manette?

LUCIE
Yes.

SOLICITOR-GEN
Are you of French birth residing in this country with your father?

LUCIE
Yes.

SOLICITOR-GEN
Have you seen the prisoner before?

LUCIE
Yes. I have visited him a few times in prison.

SOLICITOR-GEN
What was the occasion of your first meeting?

LUCIE

It was on board a packet ship, travelling from Calais to Dover, six months ago.

JUDGE

Speak up, please.

SOLICITOR-GEN

Did you have any conversation with him on that occasion?

LUCIE

Yes. I was travelling with my father, who was in a very weak state of health. Mr Darnay—

JUDGE

Do you mean the prisoner?

LUCIE

Yes, My Lord.

JUDGE

Then say the prisoner.

LUCIE

The prisoner helped me to take my father ashore. He was very kind.

SOLICITOR-GEN

When the prisoner came on board, was he alone?

LUCIE

No. Two French gentlemen were with him.

SOLICITOR-GEN

Did they confer together?

LUCIE

They talked together.

SOLICITOR-GEN

Did the prisoner hand any papers to these French gentlemen?

LUCIE

There were some papers?

SOLICITOR-GEN

(Holding up the lists) Were they like this in size and shape?

LUCIE

I—I don't know.

SOLICITOR-GEN

Come, Miss Manette. Were they like this in size and shape?

LUCIE

I can't remember.

SOLICITOR-GEN

(Patiently) Miss Manette, we all of us realise that you are giving your evidence most unwillingly, and I am sure the prisoner realises it better than anyone. But it is your duty to tell the truth. Were the papers which the prisoner handed to the two French gentlemen at Calais like this in size and shape?

LUCIE

They may have been.

SOLICITOR-GEN

They may have been. Thank you, Miss Manette.

The SOLICITOR-GENERAL *sits as* CARTON *rises.*

CARTON

Miss Manette, you say that you have visited the prisoner on frequent occasions.

LUCIE

On a few occasions, I said.

CARTON

Still, it would not be presumptuous to conclude from that that your relations with the prisoner have been friendly?

LUCIE

Yes, they have been.

CARTON

Very friendly, even?

LUCIE

Yes.

CARTON

Now, in your opinion is the prisoner capable of having committed the crime of which he is accused?

LUCIE

(With great conviction) No. I am quite sure he is innocent.

CARTON

Just one more question. Did the prisoner ever tell you why he had adopted an English name?

LUCIE

He told me that he had quarrelled with his family and was living in England because he would rather live here than anywhere else. He wishes no one to know what his real name was.

CARTON

I see. You gathered that there was nothing disgraceful about that wish for secrecy?

LUCIE

No. Certainly not.

CARTON

You gathered that it was merely due to a desire to break with the past, and to begin life afresh in a new country and under a new name?

LUCIE

Yes. I am sure that is the truth.

CARTON
Thank you, Miss Manette.

> LUCIE *goes into the anteroom.*

SOLICITOR-GEN
I call Dr Manette.

> DR MANETTE *enters the courtroom and goes into the box.*

SOLICITOR-GEN
Is your name Dr Manette?

DR MANETTE
Yes.

SOLICITOR-GEN
Are you the father of the previous witness?

DR MANETTE
I am.

SOLICITOR-GEN
Can you identify the prisoner as a fellow passenger in the Dover packet on the night of which your daughter has spoken?

DR MANETTE
No, I can't identify him.

SOLICITOR-GEN
Is there any reason why you can't do so?

DR MANETTE
There is.

SOLICITOR-GEN
Was it your misfortune that in your own country you underwent a long imprisonment, without trial or accusation?

DR MANETTE
A long imprisonment.

SOLICITOR-GEN

Had you just been released on the occasion in question?

DR MANETTE

I believe so.

SOLICITOR-GEN

Have you no remembrance of the occasion?

DR MANETTE

None whatsoever. My mind is blank from the time when I was in the Bastille to the time when I found myself living in London with my daughter. I am told that it is only quite recently that my faculties have been restored to me.

SOLICITOR-GEN

Thank you, Dr Manette.

> CARTON *does not cross-examine.* DR MANETTE *goes into the anteroom. The* SOLICITOR-GENERAL *is about to call another witness when* STRYVER *returns.*

JUDGE

(Evidently relieved) Ah, Mr Stryver. I trust you are better.

STRYVER

I thank Your Lordship, I am quite recovered.

JUDGE

I am glad you have returned. Perhaps the defence will now be conducted in a more seemly manner.

> CARTON *grins at* STRYVER. *He whispers to him, pointing out the similarity between himself and* DARNAY.

JUDGE

We will proceed.

SOLICITOR-GEN

I call Mr Jarvis Lorry.

The action moves to the anteroom. LUCIE *and* DR MANETTE *are sitting,* JERRY *is lounging against a door. A few hours have elapsed.*

LUCIE

I am sure he is innocent.

DR MANETTE

Yes, so am I. *(After a pause)* What is his secret, Lucie? Why did he change his name? Why is he living in England?

LUCIE

I only know what he has told me. He quarrelled with his family. He never told me their name. I think they are a noble family.

DR MANETTE

I wish I knew his name.

STRYVER *enters the anteroom.*

STRYVER

(Jovially) Ah, there we are.

LUCIE

Any news?

STRYVER

None as yet. The jury are still out. But that in itself is a good sign.

DR MANETTE

What do you think yourself, Mr Stryver?

STRYVER

To tell you the truth, Dr Manette, I am a little doubtful. The summing-up was so extraordinarily hostile.

DR MANETTE

It was certainly most unfair.

STRYVER

I'm told the reason for it was that His Lordship was put in a blazing bad temper by my junior's handling of the case while I was out of court. *(Chuckling)* Poor old Sydney. Always annoys the judges. That's why he's never managed to get on as well as some of us.

DR MANETTE
But it was a very clever trick. Mr Darnay and he are really extraordinarily alike.

LUCIE
I don't see that. I think he has an unpleasant face. He looks nothing like Charles.

STRYVER
Oh, come now, Miss Manette. I think that's a little hard. Perhaps he has a—shall we say—a sneaking fondness for the bottle, and shows it a little in his face. Still, he's a very good fellow at heart.

> CARTON *enters the anteroom. He has taken off his wig and gown.*

Talk of the devil. Hullo, Sydney. What have you been doing?

CARTON
Dining. *(To JERRY)* Hullo. You're the fellow who wanted to have a bet on the prisoner, aren't you? What are the odds now, do you know?

JERRY
(Looking uneasily at LUCIE) Two to one against, sir.

CARTON
I'll lay you four to one against. Will you take it?

JERRY
(Still looking at LUCIE) I—I don't know, sir.

CARTON
Ten shillings to half-a-crown?

JERRY
(Unwillingly) All right, sir.

STRYVER

Come, Sydney. It can't be as bad as that.

CARTON

After that summing-up? My dear Edward, I'm amazed they even wanted to retire.

STRYVER

You shouldn't have annoyed the judge as you did.

CARTON

Yes. *(Without emotion)* I've certainly helped to tie the noose round the prisoner's neck.

> LORRY *enters. There is a pause.*

STRYVER

Well, well, we must hope for the best. We must hope for the best.

> STRYVER *exits, whistling.*

LUCIE

(After a pause) If he should be found guilty, what will happen to him?

> *An uneasy silence follows her question.* CARTON *at length steps forward.*

CARTON

(Without emotion) He will be drawn on a hurdle to Tyburn, he will be half hanged, he will then be cut down, and—

LUCIE

(Hysterically) Stop, stop!

LORRY

Can't you see, sir, that the lady is distressed? How can you torture her by recounting these ghastly details?

CARTON

Very well, if you wish it. Miss Manette, if he is found guilty, he will be kissed on both cheeks by the judge and allowed to go home. *(He goes over to* JERRY.*)* What's your name?

JERRY

Jerry Cruncher, sir.

CARTON

Well, Jerry Cruncher, will you do something for me? Do you know the Hoop and Toy tavern opposite?

JERRY

Yes. I just been there.

CARTON

Go there for me now, will you, and bring back a bottle of their port wine. Here. *(Giving him some money)* Speak to the fair-haired potman and mention my name. He knows the brand I usually drink.

JERRY

Yes, sir.

CARTON

(Calling) And Jerry? Bring some glasses. The lady and gentlemen may care to relieve the tedium of waiting by joining me in a glass.

JERRY *leaves.* CARTON *comes back to the others.*

LORRY

We will certainly not join you, sir. How can you think of carousing at such a time as this?

CARTON

I didn't ask you to join me in a carousal, sir. I think you over-estimate the potency of the Hoop and Toy port wine.

LORRY

Sir, you are heartless.

CARTON

Sir, I am thirsty.

LUCIE

Can you feel no pity for a man in danger of his life?

CARTON

Frankly, Miss Manette, pity is an emotion I have always tried to suppress. The day before yesterday I saw a man condemned to death for stealing a few shillings. Today I may see a man condemned to death for being a Frenchman. Really, the two offences aren't so different that I should feel pity for one and not for the other. *(Bitterly)* One reason to me seems as good as another for hanging a man.

LORRY

Supposing you were in the position Charles Darnay is now? You wouldn't talk so glibly then, sir.

CARTON

I can assure you, sir, I love my life far too much to put myself in any such position.

LORRY

(Scornfully) I think that is true, sir.

CARTON

I am sure it is, sir.

> *There is a sudden excited hum from the courtroom.* CARTON *opens the courtroom door.*

The jury is coming back.

LORRY

Thank God.

> JERRY *bursts in with port and glasses.*

JERRY

Your port, sir.

> CARTON *signals to him to place it on a bench.*

JUDGE

Gentlemen of the Jury, are you agreed upon a verdict?

FOREMAN

We are.

JUDGE

Do you find the prisoner guilty or not guilty?

FOREMAN

Not guilty.

> There is a burst of cheering in the courtroom. In the anteroom,
> LUCIE is seen fainting in her father's arms.

CARTON

(His back to the MANETTES) Well, Jerry, your arrival was well-timed. Now we can have a little celebration. (Turning) What's the matter?

DR MANETTE

My daughter's unwell.

CARTON

She feels ill because he is acquitted, and yet she'd have felt just as ill if he'd been found guilty.

> CARTON kneels by LUCIE'S side, picks her up and lays her
> on a bench.

(Shouting to JERRY) I think you'd better take her home as soon as possible, sir.

DR MANETTE

Are you strong enough to walk a little?

LUCIE

(Getting to her feet) Yes, I think so. (To CARTON) Will you tell Mr Darnay that I am very very happy for his sake?

CARTON

He'll hardly need me to tell him that.

LUCIE

And tell him that we expect him this evening at our lodgings.

> CARTON *nods.*

Good-bye, Mr Carton, and thank you. I'm sorry I was so stupid as to faint.

CARTON

Not at all. As a woman you have the right to be stupid, I suppose.

LUCIE

May I say something to you, Mr Carton? I think at heart you're a very different person from what you'd have us believe.

CARTON

That's impossible. At heart I don't exist.

LUCIE

I think you do. Good-bye! Will you visit us some time?

CARTON

I should be enchanted.

> *He bows over her hand and* LUCIE *and her father go out.* CARTON *pours himself a glass of wine.* LORRY *comes out of the courtroom.*

LORRY

Where are Miss Manette and her father?

CARTON

Gone home. Miss Manette fainted.

LORRY

Good gracious! Poor thing. Why did she faint?

CARTON

It's a hot day and she's probably too tightly laced.

LORRY

I consider that a most offensive remark, sir.

CARTON

Do you, sir? Have some wine.

> LORRY *retorts with a contemptuous noise and disappears to find* LUCIE.

JERRY

(Coming over) 'Scuse me, sir. You did say ten shillings to half-a-crown, didn't you?

CARTON

I did indeed, Jerry. I'm sorry. Here. *(Giving him half-a-sovereign)* You'll be able to get drunk for a week on that.

JERRY

Not for a week, sir. Not me. Three days at most, sir. Good-bye, sir. Thank you.

> *He goes out as* STRYVER *and* DARNAY *enter the anteroom.*

STRYVER

Hullo, Sydney. Celebrating our victory, I see.

CARTON

I've made a start. *(Shaking* DARNAY'S *hand)* My very best congratulations, Mr Darnay.

DARNAY

Thank you, sir. I am very grateful for all Mr Stryver and you have done for me.

CARTON

Don't thank me. I did nothing. How does it feel to be a free man again?

DARNAY

I can't quite believe it yet. The summing-up was terrible, wasn't it? And then the waiting for the verdict. But I knew they couldn't find me guilty.

CARTON

(Sneering) You have faith in our English justice, Mr Darnay?

DARNAY

(Simply) Yes sir, I have.

STRYVER

(Sententiously) I am glad, Mr Darnay. It has always been our proud boast in this country that our trials are conducted with the strictest impartiality.

CARTON *laughs.*

DARNAY

Why do you laugh, sir? Surely my own case is an example of the truth of Mr Stryver's remark?

CARTON

I hate to destroy your illusions, Mr Darnay, but I think you owe your escape not so much to your innocence as to the exchange of smiles between you and Miss Manette when she was in the box. An English jury is never impartial, but it is always sentimental.

There is a pause. DARNAY *is uncomfortable. He looks round.*

The lady has gone home with her father. She gave me a message for you. I was to tell you that your release had made her very happy, and that she and her father expect you this evening at their lodgings.

DARNAY

I see. Thank you. You're very kind, all of you. I suppose I am quite free to go now. I must say good-bye, then, and again, I am more grateful than I can express.

CARTON

You must have one glass of wine with me before you go.

He goes to fetch a glass.

DARNAY
Well—

CARTON
(Over his shoulder) You, too, Edward. We must pledge Mr Darnay's health.

STRYVER
An excellent idea, Sydney.

      CARTON *pours out three glasses of wine.*

(To DARNAY*)* A charming young lady, Miss Manette. Charming.

DARNAY
(Stiffly) I'm glad you think so.

CARTON
(Returning with the glasses) Was even your wizened old heart touched by the sight of beauty in distress, Edward?

STRYVER
It was, Sydney, it was. I believe yours was too, though you'd be ashamed to admit it.

CARTON
Do you think that, Edward? Do you think I'd be ashamed to admit it? *(He hands him a glass and then turns to* DARNAY.*)* Here, Mr Darnay. Now, sir, will you give us a toast?

DARNAY
A toast, sir? What toast?

CARTON
I leave that to you.

DARNAY
(After a pause) Very well. To Lucie Manette.

STRYVER

To Lucie Manette.

CARTON

To Lucie Manette.

> *They all drink.* CARTON, *looking straight at* DARNAY, *hurls his glass over his shoulder against the wall. There is a pause.*

CARTON

(At length) You must go, Mr Darnay, or you'll be late.

> DARNAY *seems about to say something, checks himself, bows stiffly and walks across to the door.* STRYVER *disapproves of* CARTON'S *behaviour and exits.* CARTON *moves to* DARNAY'S *glass of wine, which isn't finished, and drinks it before exiting.*

> *End of Act One.*

ACT TWO

SCENE ONE

DR MANETTE'S *lodgings in Soho.*

A small, pleasantly furnished room, with French windows and steps leading down into the garden. DARNAY stands behind LUCIE as she plays; DR MANETTE and LORRY sit, sipping cups of tea. MISS PROSS sits near a large tea-urn and CARTON leans against the window with his back to the room.

LUCIE sings a song. When she has finished the others applaud. All except CARTON make murmurs of praise.

LORRY

Charming, my dear. Charming.

LUCIE

Thank you, Mr Lorry.

> *She continues to play gently.*

LORRY

(Rather sharply) Didn't you enjoy that, Carton?

CARTON

(Without turning) It was delightful.

LORRY

What a joy it is to be in England and to be able to come to these enchanting Sunday afternoons of yours again. Such a change after these last two months.

DR MANETTE

We have missed you, my dear Lorry. I trust your bank will not be sending you abroad again for a long time.

LORRY

I trust not—at least, not to Paris.

MISS PROSS

(With a sniff) Paris! You're well out of that city, Mr Lorry, believe me.

LORRY

I quite agree with you, Miss Pross. There was a time when I used to enjoy being sent out there. But not any longer. It is a haunted city.

DR MANETTE

Haunted? By what?

LORRY

By fear, Doctor.

DR MANETTE

Fear of tyranny?

LORRY

Yes, but even more—fear of what may happen when the tyranny falls, as—mark me, Doctor—fall it will. France is bankrupt and rotten with corruption. Something—and something terrible—is bound to happen soon. Believe me when I say the atmosphere over there is enough to chill one to the marrow.

MISS PROSS

(In his ear) More tea?

LORRY

(Startled) Eh? What's that? Oh, thank you, Miss Pross, no.

DR MANETTE

It is really too pleasant an afternoon to waste talking politics indoors. Come and play me a game of chess in the garden, Lorry.

LORRY

Delighted.

DR MANETTE

You must come and advise me, Carton. Lorry is rather too good for me, I have to admit.

CARTON

Heavens, no. Far too hot to move.

> DR MANETTE *and* LORRY *go into the garden.* LUCIE *takes* DARNAY'S *hand, he whispers something to her, and she laughs.* CARTON *watches them. Once they realise they are alone in the room with him, they excuse themselves to stroll in the garden.* CARTON *turns to* MISS PROSS, *playing with his empty glass meaningfully.*

MISS PROSS

Oh no, you don't. Not a drop more. You ought to be ashamed of yourself drinking wine on a Sunday afternoon. What's the matter with tea, I'd like to know.

CARTON

A revolting beverage. And very bad for the nerves.

> MISS PROSS *picks up the tea-urn.*

MISS PROSS

(As she moves to the door) Let me tell you, young man, it would do you a power of good if you were made to drink tea and nothing else all day long for the rest of your life.

CARTON

I suppose that's what my punishment will be in the next world.

MISS PROSS

It'll be something far worse than that, don't you worry.

> *She goes out.* CARTON *takes a decanter from the sideboard, and is pouring himself a glass when* MISS PROSS *returns.*

Aha! Caught in the very act.

She snatches the decanter away.

CARTON

Oh, please, Miss Pross. It's for my health.

MISS PROSS

What's the matter with your health?

CARTON

I feel very faint.

    MISS PROSS *gives him back the decanter unwillingly.*

CARTON

Won't you join me?

MISS PROSS

The idea! Not but what I haven't more need of it than you.

    There is a ring at the front door.

Lord, now, who can that be? The place is becoming a positive coffee-house.

    She goes out.

STRYVER

(Off) Ah, Miss Pross, is your mistress in?

MISS PROSS

(Off) I can't say whether she is or she isn't. But you'd better come in now that you're here.

    STRYVER *enters, followed by* MISS PROSS. STRYVER *is elaborately dressed and carries a bouquet of flowers, which he hides behind his back.*

CARTON

Edward, by all that's wonderful! And dressed like a fashion-plate. *(He looks down at his own shabby clothes.)* You put me to shame, my dear fellow. I must go home.

STRYVER

(Irritably) Nonsense, Sydney. This is quite an old suit. Nothing out of the ordinary at all. Er—Miss Pross, pray tell your mistress I have called.

> MISS PROSS, *who has been giggling at* STRYVER'S *appearance, sweeps him a deep curtsey.*

MISS PROSS

I fly to obey, Your Lordship.

> *She runs out.*

STRYVER

What an insolent creature that is!

> CARTON *is staring at him, entranced.*

Well, well, Sydney. There's nothing to stare at, is there?

CARTON

Forgive me, Edward. My eyes are dazzled by such magnificence. Have a glass of the good doctor's Madeira—that is, if you're not ashamed to drink with so meanly a dog as myself.

> *He pours* STRYVER *a glass of wine and then raises his own.*

(Toasting) Beau Stryver!

STRYVER

Tush! Your clowning is tedious, Sydney.

> *In drinking, he spills some of his wine.*

CARTON

What the devil is the matter with you, Edward?

STRYVER

(On an impulse) Sydney, you can be discreet, can't you?

CARTON

As the grave.

STRYVER

Then I'll tell you something that will surprise you. Sydney, I intend to marry.

CARTON

Well, well!

STRYVER

Yes, and not for money. Now what do you say? Well, aren't you surprised?

CARTON

I am struck dumb, Edward! I simply have no words to express my astonishment! It's only now that I begin to realise the full implication of your news. If you're not marrying for money, you must be marrying for love. Now that is a truly portentous thought!

STRYVER

I might have expected that sort of dismal cynicism from you, Sydney—I must speak strongly to you. You're the most insensitive, boorish, ungallant dog that ever lived. You've never had an ounce of true feeling in your life. How often have you come here with me to Dr Manette's lodgings and sat in a corner with a sheepish hang-dog look on your face? You rarely open your mouth, and when you do, it's always to be rude to someone: and, above all, you're extremely disagreeable to our charming hostess—Miss Manette. Now, why do you think I get on in my life and my profession, while you remain stationary?

CARTON

I don't think you do get on. I go backwards, and that gives you the impression that you're going forwards.

STRYVER

(With venom) I haven't the time to waste in arguing with you. You're incorrigible.

CARTON

You haven't told me yet who the lady is.

STRYVER

You know her. In fact, you are under her roof at the moment.

CARTON

Good heavens! Miss Pross!

STRYVER

(Furiously) No, not Miss Pross. Miss Manette. *(Defiantly, after a pause)* Well, what do you say?

CARTON

I say nothing. Nothing at all.

STRYVER

She's a charming young lady. No money, of course, still, I don't think I need to consider that. She'll have in me a husband who is already well off, and may one day be very rich—very rich indeed, in spite of what you say. Yes. I think we are both to be congratulated.

CARTON

Undoubtedly. Especially of the young lady. What an astonishing piece of good fortune for her!

STRYVER

Well, I think she deserves some good fortune after all she's been through. Anyway, I've made up my mind and I'm going to marry and settle down: and, incidentally, I strongly advise you to do the same. Find some good respectable matron with a little money—a landlady, say—and marry her against a rainy day. That's what you ought to do. Think of it, Sydney!

CARTON

I'll think of it.

STRYVER

Do.

    LUCIE *enters, followed by* MISS PROSS.

LUCIE

Mr Stryver! How good of you to come and see us. We weren't expecting you.

STRYVER

(With an elaborate bow) I trust my intrusion is not distasteful to you, my dear young lady.

> *He kisses her hand.* LUCIE *smiles at* CARTON *over the top of* STRYVER'S *head.*

LUCIE

(Insincerely) What an absurd idea!

> STRYVER, *stands with the bouquet behind his back, glaring at* CARTON. MISS PROSS *is clearing away the remaining tea-things.* STRYVER *coughs meaningfully.* CARTON, *who has been gazing at the ceiling, pretends to catch his meaning suddenly and to be confused at his obtuseness. He finishes his wine hurriedly.*

STRYVER

Sydney, my dear fellow, perhaps you'd like to take a short stroll in the garden?

CARTON

Delighted, sir, I'm sure.

MISS PROSS

Wouldn't you like to take the decanter with you?

CARTON

No. So long as I know where it is, I have no immediate regrets at leaving it.

> *He goes out to the garden. After a look from* STRYVER, MISS PROSS *goes to the kitchen.*

LUCIE

Won't you sit down?

> STRYVER *bows and remains standing.* LUCIE *sits.*

STRYVER

(Producing his bouquet) Miss Manette—here is a trifling token of esteem and regard from your humble servant and most devoted slave.

He hands her the bouquet.

LUCIE

(Nervously) It is very kind of you, Mr Stryver. Very kind of you indeed.

> *There is a pause as* STRYVER *meditates on how to begin. He slowly and cumbrously settles himself on one knee. Once he is comfortable, he takes* LUCIE'S *hand and addresses her rather as if she were a judge.*

STRYVER

Miss Manette—Lucie, if I may so address you...

> LUCIE *nods nervously, and is about to speak, but* STRYVER *continues remorselessly.*

I must beg of you to listen to the communication I am going to make to you with the greatest attention, for it touches both of us very nearly. Now...

LUCIE

(Unkindly) Forgive me, Mr Stryver, but—don't you find that position a little uncomfortable? Wouldn't you prefer a chair. *(She indicates a chair.)*

STRYVER

Thank you, I am perfectly comfortable. Now—Miss Manette—I mean—Lucie, you see before you a man, who, I think I may say without undue self-glorification, has achieved a certain measure of success. Lately, however, it has been borne in upon this man... that there is one thing above all that he lacks—by which I mean companion with whom to share his remaining days, a fellow-traveller on the journey of life—if I may coin a phrase. Now, this man is not a man to make a light choice...

LUCIE

(Rising) I take it, Mr Stryver, that you are proposing marriage to me.

STRYVER

(Testily) That was my intention, but I would rather you heard me out, Miss Manette—Lucie.

LUCIE

Forgive me, but there is really no need. It is embarrassing for me, and probably very exhausting for you.

STRYVER *rises.*

STRYVER

Embarrassing?

LUCIE

You see, Mr Stryver, grateful and—er—flattered as I am by your—er—kind proposal—I fear I am not free to accept it.

STRYVER

Not free? *(He stares down at her unbelievingly.)* Who is the man?

LUCIE

I'd rather you didn't ask that. It is still a secret. Even my father doesn't know. You see, the man I am going to marry is not a man of substance like you, Mr Stryver. He has practically no money at all.

STRYVER

No money at all? My dear young lady, you have been most cruelly used. However, you mustn't fret. Such an engagement can easily be broken.

LUCIE *bursts out laughing.*

STRYVER

What is the joke?

LUCIE

(Laughing) You, Mr Stryver.

STRYVER

(Horrified) Me?

LUCIE

I'm sorry. *(Controlling herself)* You see, I really have no intention of breaking my engagement. In fact, it now looks as if we are going to be married quite soon. I have just heard that my betrothed has come into a small legacy, and that, with his school-teacher's salary, should be enough...

STRYVER

School-teacher? No, by God, it can't be!

LUCIE

Please, Mr Stryver, if you have guessed who it is, do keep our secret for a little longer.

STRYVER

Darnay! So that's who it is. Darnay!

> DARNAY *enters.*

DARNAY

(Affably) Did you call me, sir?

LUCIE

Charles! You've been listening?

DARNAY

An unworthy suspicion, my dear.

> *Enter* CARTON *and* DR MANETTE *from the garden.*

DR MANETTE

I should never have let him take my castle. I'm afraid he's much too good for me. Why, Stryver, I never knew you were here!

> STRYVER *does not answer.*

LUCIE

Won't you come into the garden with us, Mr Stryver?

STRYVER

(Furiously) Thank you, madam, but I must take my leave.

> MISS PROSS *comes in from the hall, as if she had been summoned.*

MISS PROSS

Mr Stryver's hat and stick.

> MISS PROSS *goes to open the front door.*

LUCIE

Good-bye, Mr Stryver.

STRYVER

(Bowing stiffly) Good-bye, Madam.

> LUCIE *and* DARNAY *go out into the garden.* LORRY *can be seen outside, talking to* LUCIE *and* DARNAY. MISS PROSS *goes out.*

DR MANETTE

You're not leaving us, I trust, Stryver?

STRYVER

(Turning) I AM leaving you, sir. What is more, I very much doubt if I shall ever set foot in your house again.

CARTON

(Quietly) Don't be an idiot, Edward.

DR MANETTE

Why, what on earth is the matter?

STRYVER

This is the matter, sir. I do not like to be made a fool of.

DR MANETTE

No, indeed. Nor do I. But—

STRYVER

Furthermore, I consider that a father who allows his daughter to become entangled with a penniless adventurer has lamentably failed in his duty.

> CARTON *moves quickly up to* STRYVER.

CARTON

Edward—I think you had better go.

DR MANETTE

(Brushing CARTON *aside)* I must ask you to explain yourself.

STRYVER

I see no need to do so. I merely consider that a pettifogging little school-teacher, of doubtful foreign extraction and a former gaolbird, is hardly a suitable match for your daughter, mincing little wanton though she is.

> CARTON *hits* STRYVER *in the face.* STRYVER *glares at him for a moment, then turns abruptly and goes.* CARTON *stares after him.*

CARTON

I'm ashamed of myself.

DR MANETTE

Ashamed? You acted as any gentleman should.

CARTON

I'm not a gentleman, and God forbid I should ever act like one. With that gesture I've wrecked what little livelihood I've got. *(He collects his hat and stick from the corner of the room.)* I must ask you one thing, sir. Please say nothing of this incident to your daughter.

DR MANETTE

Very well, if you wish it.

CARTON

Goodbye, then. Please pay my respects to the others.

> *He moves to the door.*

DR MANETTE

Carton—

> CARTON *turns.*

What Stryver said—about Lucie and Charles—he meant Charles of course—is it true?

CARTON

I've no idea. *(Sincerely)* If it is, I wish them both every happiness. Good-bye, sir.

> *He goes out.* DR MANETTE *goes to the window.*

DR MANETTE

Lucie—Charles! Come here, please.

>LUCIE *appears at the window, followed by* DARNAY.

LUCIE

Yes, father?

DR MANETTE

Lucie, my dear, I beg of you to tell me the truth. Are you and Charles engaged to be married?

LUCIE

Oh, Father, I'm so sorry you should have heard from that horrible man.

DARNAY

Believe me, Dr Manette, we had no wish to practise any deceit: it was merely that until I was in a position to offer your daughter something more than a mere school-teacher's allowance, I was not going to ask you formally for her hand in marriage.

LUCIE

But now it's different, Father. Charles has had a legacy from abroad.

DARNAY

It is not large, but sufficient, I think, to give your daughter a comfortable home.

DR MANETTE

I see.

>*He sinks slowly into a chair.*

LUCIE

Oh, Father. You're not angry with us? You will give your consent, won't you?

>DR MANETTE *strokes her hair but says nothing.*

DARNAY

Dr Manette, I know that before you give me an answer—before you decide either for me or against me—there's a question I shall have to answer and I intend to do it. You will want to know who I am and what my real name is.

DR MANETTE

(Rising, violently) No. No. I don't want to know.

DARNAY

(Puzzled) But I must tell you my story, sir. It's only right.

DR MANETTE

Right? I don't care if it's right. I don't want to know.

DR MANETTE *laughs.*

(Harshly) I know your story. I know your name. You are Charles Darnay.

DARNAY

I am Charles St. Evrémonde, nephew of the Marquis de St. Evrémonde.

DR MANETTE *moves to his shoemaker's cobble, and commences working as in Act One, Scene One.*

I quarrelled with my father on a matter of—politics. I had never intended to go back to France again. But my father died a few weeks ago, and I am leaving very soon to see my uncle. He wants to make a reconciliation, so that the name of Evrémonde shall not die out, but I am going to tell him that I renounce any claim I may have to the title and the property. If your daughter marries me, she will be Mrs Charles Darnay.

DR MANETTE *does not appear to be listening. He stops for a moment then continues working.*

That's what I wanted you to know, sir. Does it make any difference?

DR MANETTE

(Looking up) What?

DARNAY

I asked you if what I've told you about myself will make any difference.

DR MANETTE

No. No difference.

DARNAY

I hope nothing I've said has distressed you, sir. I fear this must have been a shock to you.

DR MANETTE

(Struggling to focus on DARNAY*)* A shock? I don't think it was a shock. You have my consent—both of you—God bless you both—may you be very happy.

DARNAY

Thank you, sir. Oh, thank you.

LUCIE

Oh, Father!

DR MANETTE

It's all right, child. Now leave me, both of you. Lorry will be feeling deserted.

LUCIE

(Doubtfully) Are you sure you are feeling all right, Father?

DR MANETTE

Leave me, please.

LUCIE

Very well. Come, Charles.

> DARNAY *squeezes her arm and together they go out.* DR MANETTE *presses his hand to his head. He mutters furtively to himself as he works.*
>
> *End of scene.*

Scene Two

Exterior and interior of DEFARGE'S *wine shop in the Place de St. Antoine, Paris. Late afternoon, two weeks later.*

The shop is located in the middle of a busy intersection of many roads, a place for the community to meet, trade and talk. The windows are open, people are coming and going.

MADAME DEFARGE *stands behind the counter, cutting slices off a long loaf of bread. A* CHILD, *about six years old and clutching a doll, watches her with intent pleasure.* MADAME DEFARGE *stops cutting and turns to fetch a plate. The* CHILD *grasps the bread knife, trying to imitate her actions.* MADAME DEFARGE *watches for a second with an amused smile, then takes the knife from the* CHILD *and shows her how it should be done. The* CHILD *holds out her doll to* MADAME DEFARGE *who, laughing delightedly, makes as if to cut off its head. She gives the* CHILD *a piece of bread, and pats it on the head. She then sits down and resumes her knitting.*

People are sitting about, gossiping in the street and at the windows. GASPARD *sits at a table, drinking a glass of wine.* DEFARGE *enters.*

DEFARGE

Hello, little lady! What's that you're eating? A piece of bread? Aren't you lucky? *(To* GASPARD*)* Well, not much for the children to eat these days.

GASPARD *shrugs his shoulders and gives the* CHILD *wine on his finger.* MADAME DEFARGE *brings two glasses of wine, and the men sit round the table outside the shop.* MADAME DEFARGE *sits in a rocking chair by the door, knitting. The* CHILD *plays in the street.*

GASPARD

I've brought some news.

DEFARGE

Important?

GASPARD *nods.*

GASPARD

There's been a new police spy commissioned to this quarter. I heard for certain last night.

DEFARGE

Do you know his name?

GASPARD

He's an Englishman. Name of Barsad. John Barsad. About forty, dark, long nose, rather bald, and a small scar on the left cheek.

DEFARGE

Quite a portrait. *(To* MADAME DEFARGE *who is still knitting in her rocking chair)* Did you hear that, Thérèse?

MADAM DEFARGE *nods and continues knitting.*

DEFARGE

If he comes into the shop, give the signal.

MADAME DEFARGE *takes a rose from her belt and holds it to her hair.*

B.A.R.S.A.D. It won't be hard to knit.

GASPARD

I often wonder if that really is the best way of keeping the register. After all, everyone can see your wife knitting. Surely she ought to be more careful?

DEFARGE

Don't worry, Gaspard. It's quite safe. Only Thérèse can decipher it.

GASPARD

But—I don't like to say it—but still, if she were to die—

DEFARGE

The register would be lost. But Thérèse won't die, Gaspard. You'll outlive us all, won't you, my dear? *(He kisses her head.)* I sometimes think that you'll be the only one of us who lives to see the day.

GASPARD

We'll all live to see it. Don't say you're losing heart, Jacques. It will come some time.

DEFARGE

(Bitterly) That's an old story. When?

GASPARD

(Shrugging his shoulders) Next year, perhaps.

DEFARGE

We said that last year. We've been saying it for twenty years. But is it any nearer? I saw them today—the pudding-faced King and his harlot of a Queen, riding out of Versailles with their lords and ladies, as proud, as secure, as scornful of us all as ever they were.

> *The men sit, silent and depressed.* MADAME DEFARGE *continues to knit. From the back of the narrow street comes a coach, which has some difficultly getting through. The coachman, lashing out on both sides with his whip, clears a passage and whips up the horses.*
>
> *Simultaneously, The* CHILD *runs out into the street. The coach appears to run her down. There is a sudden scream, a clatter as the coach pulls up, and a babble of voices as a crowd collects.* GASPARD *forces his way through them, screams, and reappears with the dead* CHILD *in his arms. He lays the body beside the fountain and bathes its forehead. The crowd murmurs, shaking their fists at the coach.*
>
> GABELLE *comes down from the box. Out of the coach steps the* MARQUIS DE ST. EVREMONDE.

MARQUIS

(Looking round, distastefully) What has gone wrong?

GABELLE

Pardon, Monseigneur, it is a child—

> GASPARD *wails.*

MARQUIS

Why does he make that abominable noise? Is it his child?

> GABELLE *nods.*

Hm. That explains, if it does not excuse, a most unpleasing sound. Is the child badly hurt?

GABELLE

I believe so, Monseigneur.

MARQUIS

(Looking round) It is extraordinary to me that you people cannot take more care of yourselves and your children. How do I know what injury you have done my horses? *(A pause)* Who is in charge here?

> DEFARGE *steps forward. The* MARQUIS *takes a coin from his purse.*

Give that to the child's father. And you may bring me a glass of wine.

> MADAME DEFARGE *pours out a glass at the table in front of the shop, and passes it to* DEFARGE, *who brings it to him.*

(Spluttering) I asked for wine. What is this devilish concoction you have given me?

DEFARGE

Wine, Monseigneur, the best I have in my shop.

MARQUIS

May the good Lord preserve me from your worst. Take this away. It is really beyond a joke. *(He turns to get into the carriage again.)*

GASPARD runs towards the carriage. The MARQUIS *swings round, with his hand on his sword hilt.* DEFARGE *holds* GASPARD *back.*

GASPARD

She's dead. My daughter's dead!

DEFARGE

Poor Gaspard. I'm very sorry.

      GASPARD *looks at him blankly.*

You remember, the day when your daughter was born, I told you I pitied her. Now she's dead in a moment without pain. That's your comfort, Gaspard. She couldn't have lived an hour as happily.

MARQUIS

(Genially) Ah. A philosopher, I see. What's your name, Monsieur Wineshopkeeper?

DEFARGE

My name is Defarge, Monsieur de St. Evrémonde.

MARQUIS

You know me?

DEFARGE

I know you, Monseigneur le Marquis.

MARQUIS

(Pleased) Well, Monsieur Defarge, you have amused me with your quaint philosophy. *(Throwing him a coin)* Pick that up and spend it as you like.

    The MARQUIS *gets into the coach,* GABELLE *goes to mount the box and the crowd surround the coach. The coin is thrown at the window. The door of the coach opens and the* MARQUIS *appears.*

(Without anger) Who threw that coin?

    No one answers. The MARQUIS *looks round. His eyes rest on* MADAME DEFARGE, *standing knitting.*

You dogs! I would gladly ride over any of you and exterminate you from the earth. If I knew which rascal threw at the carriage, he should be crushed under the wheels.

> *The* MARQUIS *gets into the coach, assisted by* GABELLE. *The coach moves off. Some of the crowd run after the coach.* MADAME DEFARGE *stands by the* CHILD'S *body, knitting.*

MAN

Filthy swine of an aristocrat! May he rot in hell!

> MADAME DEFARGE *looks sharply at the* MAN *who has spoken. She puts a rose in her hair. He is revealed to be* BARSAD.

BARSAD

What is that you are knitting, Madame? May I see it?

> MADAME DEFARGE *holds it up for him to see. He takes it in his hand and examines it. After a moment, she takes it back and recommences knitting.*

Your wife knits very fast, Monsieur Defarge.

DEFARGE

She has a good deal to do.

BARSAD

What does she make?

DEFARGE

Many things.

BARSAD

For instance...?

DEFARGE

For instance—shrouds.

BARSAD

(A pause) Well, it's interesting to meet you, Madame Defarge, because we have a mutual friend.

MADAME DEFARGE *looks up.*

Dr Alexandre Manette.

A pause. She stops smiling.

His daughter is engaged to be married. Oddly enough, to the nephew of our friend who was in just now—the Marquis de St. Evrémonde. In England he has taken the name of Charles Darnay. But in spite of that he is the legal heir. So your friend's daughter will one day be the Marquise de St. Evrémonde. I thought it might interest you to know that.

MADAME DEFARGE *nods slowly and resumes her knitting.*

Well, I must be off. Goodbye, Madame. I shall come again soon.

BARSAD *goes out.*

End of scene.

SCENE THREE

The MARQUIS' *bedroom in his Château at Beauvais. Very late on the same summer night as Scene Two.*

Enter the MARQUIS, *followed by* GABELLE *and* VALET.

MARQUIS

I gather that my nephew has not arrived?

GABELLE

Not yet, Monseigneur le Marquis.

MARQUIS

Then he may not arrive tonight. If he does, I wish you to tell him that I await him here. I shall begin my supper without him.

GABELLE

Very well, Monseigneur le Marquis.

MARQUIS

That is all, Monsieur Gabelle.

>   GABELLE *does not go. After a pause, he coughs to attract the* MARQUIS' *attention.*

Yes? Yes? What is it now?

GABELLE

If it please you, Monseigneur, there is a fellow, a road-mender—

who has come to the Château tonight with a very strange story. I
think you should hear it.

MARQUIS

My dear Monsieur Gabelle, I am always ready to listen to a good
story. But surely this is hardly the time or the place for the exchange
of anecdotes with a road-mender? If I am to have entertainment, I
should prefer some music. Tell them to entertain me while I have
my supper.

GABELLE *motions to the* VALET *who goes.*

GABELLE

If it please you, Monseigneur, I think it is very important that you
should see this road-mender. He is outside now. May I beg you to
hear what he has to say?

MARQUIS

I see you are in one of your obstinate moods tonight, Monsieur
Gabelle. I shall have no peace, I suppose, until I see him. Bring
him in.

GABELLE *goes to the door and beckons. The* ROAD-
MENDER *comes in and stands before the* MARQUIS
fidgeting with his cap.

Well? I hear you have something to tell me.

ROAD-MENDER

Yes, Monseigneur le Marquis.

MARQUIS

(After a pause) I am waiting.

ROAD-MENDER

Well, Monseigneur le Marquis, it was like this, you see.

MARQUIS

Like what?

GABELLE

Tell your story properly. There's no need to be frightened.

ROAD-MENDER

Well, Monseigneur le Marquis, I was working this afternoon on the Paris road, when you passed me in your coach—I mean, you did me the honour to drive past me, Monseigneur le Marquis, and that was when I saw the man.

MARQUIS

A man. How interesting. What a strange thing to see on the Paris road. What was the man doing? Standing on his head, I suppose?

ROAD-MENDER

(Grinning) Yes, he was, in a manner of speaking. In a manner of speaking, that's just what he was doing, standing on his head.

The MARQUIS looks appealingly at GABELLE.

He was hanging by the drag-chain under your coach.

MARQUIS
(Sharply) What?

ROAD-MENDER

Like this, he was. (He throws his head back and grasps an imaginary chain.)

MARQUIS

Hanging by the chain? But he would have been suffocated. Who was this man?

ROAD-MENDER

I don't know, Monseigneur le Marquis. He didn't come from hereabouts. That I'll be bound.

MARQUIS
What did he look like?

ROAD-MENDER

Like a ghost. White as a ghost. All covered with dust, he was.

MARQUIS

(After a pause) I think, Monsieur Road-mender, that you had too much to drink this afternoon.

The ROAD-MENDER *starts to protest.*

Take him away, Monsieur Gabelle, and leave me to have my supper in peace.

GABELLE *and the* ROAD-MENDER *go out.*

(To a LACKEY*)* Are the musicians there?

LACKEY

Yes, Monseigneur.

MARQUIS

Tell them to play.

The MARQUIS *looks out of the window. After a while* GABELLE *comes back.*

GABELLE

May it please you, Monseigneur, your nephew has this moment arrived.

MARQUIS

An unpardonable hour. He must have learnt such manners from his friends, the English. Have you told him to attend me here?

GABELLE

He is on his way up, Monseigneur le Marquis.

DARNAY *comes in. The* MARQUIS *rises and they bow to each other very formally.*

MARQUIS

My dear nephew, I cannot tell you how delighted I am to see you. You've been a long time coming.

DARNAY

On the contrary, I come direct.

MARQUIS

Pardon me! I mean, not a long time on the journey, a long time intending the journey.

DARNAY

I have been detained by—various business—

MARQUIS

Without doubt.

> GABELLE *comes forward and relieves* DARNAY *of his top-coat.*

MARQUIS

You and my agent, Monsieur Gabelle, are already good friends, I believe.

DARNAY

I am very happy to meet you again, my dear Gabelle.

GABELLE

You are too kind, Monsieur de St. Evrémonde.

MARQUIS

(Interrupting) You may leave us now, Monsieur Gabelle. Stop the music, and dismiss the servants. Send Francois here in a half an hour. Good-night.

GABELLE

Good-night, Monseigneur le Marquis, Good-night, Monsieur de St. Evrémonde.

> GABELLE *goes. The* MARQUIS *bows* DARNAY *into a chair, and then sits down himself.*

MARQUIS

I hear that, in England, you were in some danger of being hanged as a spy. Rather an uncomfortable check to your enthusiasm, I should have thought.

DARNAY

I doubt, sir, that if I had been on the very brink of death, you would have cared to stir a finger to prevent it. Indeed, for all I know, you may have worked expressly to give a more suspicious character to the circumstances that surrounded me.

MARQUIS

Yes, it is possible. For the honour of the family I might even have ventured to incommode you to that extent. Please excuse me.

DARNAY *bows ironically.*

I have long believed that the administration of a little—shall we say—solitude, would mould your character to great advantage. In short I think it would make another man of you.

DARNAY

I have no doubt it would.

MARQUIS

However, I have admittedly failed in my efforts on your behalf, so there is no use in discussing the question further. All is changed for the worse these days. A few years ago—why, men have been taken out to be hanged from this very room. One fellow, to my knowledge, was poniarded on the spot for making some insolent protestations with regard to his daughter—HIS daughter! We have lost many privileges—a new philosophy has become the mode—bad, very bad.

DARNAY

The new philosophy distresses you, Uncle.

MARQUIS

No. All that distresses me is that it should be read by minds incapable of appreciating it. But that you—and such as you—should read it and believe in it, does not distress me in the least. Philosophy, after all, is or should be, the birthright of our class.

DARNAY

Rousseau has written "Man is born free and is everywhere in chains".

MARQUIS

Exactly. The phrase in question I find in intolerable taste, and anyway so obviously true that it need never have been written.

DARNAY

True? You believe it true? Then why are you content to do nothing about it?

MARQUIS

What can one do about it? What remedy does the author of the phrase suggest himself? That we should revert to a state of nature. A state of nature! How very uncomfortable. And how very draughty in the cold weather. No. I am happier as I am in my present unregenerate state.

DARNAY

YOU are happier as you are. Yes. But what about the peasants starving in the gutter?

MARQUIS

Ah. What about them? Have some wine.

DARNAY

Strangely enough, a man I know in London made me almost precisely the same answer the other day. It is an attitude that I find quite despicable.

MARQUIS

It is the right attitude. It is certainly the only reasonable attitude.

DARNAY

I hate reason.

MARQUIS

It is a pity, then, that you live in an age of reason.

DARNAY

The age of reason is passed, or at least is passing quickly.

MARQUIS

Really? And what is going to take its place?

DARNAY

The age of brotherhood—the brotherhood of all men.

MARQUIS

What an infinitely depressing prospect. Have you never thought, Charles, how dull and flat a thing equality is? If this age of yours ever comes, what an irreparable loss humanity will suffer.

DARNAY

What loss?

MARQUIS

(With a wide gesture embracing the room) This, for instance. It has meaning, Charles. *(Taking snuff)* I think one day you will understand that. You must remember that equality does not mean raising the valley to the level of the hill, it means lowering the hill to the level of the valley. That is badly expressed, but I think you will understand what I am trying to say.

DARNAY

I understand, but I certainly do not approve.

MARQUIS

If you do not approve, I do not think you fully understand. One day, as I say, perhaps you will. When you are the Marquis de St. Evrémonde—

DARNAY

(Rising) I shall never be the Marquis de St. Evrémonde.

MARQUIS

Supposing I were to die tonight, Charles, a contingency which I venture to think unlikely—still, let us suppose—then you would be the Marquis de St. Evrémonde.

DARNAY

I came here to tell you that I renounce for all time any claim to the title or the property, or even to French citizenship. I intend to live in England under the name of Charles Darnay.

MARQUIS

The name of Evrémonde would be gone for ever.

DARNAY

I am content that it should. It is the worst-hated name in all France.

MARQUIS

Let us hope so. Detestation of the high is the involuntary homage of the low. *(Rising)* Well, well. There is no point in continuing this argument further tonight. You are probably tired after your journey and would like to go to bed.

DARNAY

I should tell you I am to be married shortly.

MARQUIS

Ah, I thought so. I noticed a strange glitter in your eye which I believed to be not entirely due to revolutionary ardour. Who is the fortunate lady?

DARNAY

She is the daughter of a French doctor, living in exile like myself.

MARQUIS

(Picking up a glass of wine) The name?

DARNAY

Her name is Manette.

> The MARQUIS *stops his glass half way to his lips. He puts it down slowly.*

MARQUIS

Send my valet. *(Turning, his composure regained)* Good-night, Charles. We shall continue our discussion in the morning. Good repose.

DARNAY

Good-night, Monseigneur.

MARQUIS

(To a LACKEY *offstage)* Light my nephew to his room.

> *They bow formally.* DARNAY *goes out. The* MARQUIS *stands in meditation. After a while he laughs shortly and yawns.*

(Pleasantly) And burn my nephew in his bed if you will.

> *The* VALET *enters and bows low. The* VALET *goes to the door.*

Tell me, François. Do you read Rousseau?

VALET

I do, Monseigneur.

MARQUIS

What is your opinion of him?

VALET

A pretentious bore, Monseigneur.

MARQUIS

In my pocket you will find three louis. You may take one.

> *He reaches into his pocket to retrieve the coins.*

VALET

Monseigneur is too kind.

MARQUIS

Where did you learn that phrase, pretentious bore?

VALET

From yourself, Monseigneur. That was how you once described him to me.

MARQUIS

I shall not ask you to put that louis back, François. In fact, you may take another for your good memory.

VALET

Monseigneur overwhelms me.

He reaches deeper into his pocket.

MARQUIS

Am I a good master, François?

VALET

None better, Monseigneur.

MARQUIS

And yet you hate me as much as anyone.

VALET

Monseigneur—

MARQUIS

Don't protest, François. I thrive on hatred. There is a third louis in my pocket. Had you been honest it might have been yours. Good-night, François.

VALET

Good-night, Monseigneur.

> *The* VALET *bows himself out of the bedchamber. He takes the candles out, leaving the room in darkness, save for a glimmer of light from the window. Silence. Darkness.* GASPARD *enters. He walks to the sleeping* MARQUIS *and watches him. He has with him his dead* CHILD'S *doll. He kisses the doll and then suffocates the* MARQUIS *to death.*
>
> *End of scene.*

SCENE FOUR

DR MANETTE'S *lodgings in Soho. Three months later. Evening, about six o'clock.*

LUCIE *is dressed in her wedding dress. The shoemaker's bench can no longer be seen in the room. She looks at herself in the mirror. The front door bell rings. She goes eagerly to open it.*

LUCIE

(Off, her voice betraying disappointment) Oh, it's you, Mr Carton.

CARTON

(Off) If I'm a nuisance, please send me away.

LUCIE

No, no. Of course not. Please come in.

> *She comes into the room,* CARTON *following.*

Well! Do you like it? I've been showing Father how I shall look tomorrow.

CARTON

You're sure I'm not disturbing you?

LUCIE

No, no, it's nice to see you. Prossie's out finishing her shopping.

CARTON

Is your father quite recovered?

LUCIE

Oh yes, he seems to be perfectly well again. I've persuaded him to go to bed early so as to be fresh for tomorrow.

CARTON

My excuse for coming so late was to bring you a small wedding present. *(He hands her a little box.)* I'm afraid it hardly even deserves that name.

LUCIE

(Opening box) Oh, but it's charming. *(She takes out a gold brooch which CARTON has worn in his cravat in previous scenes.)* It's charming. Thank you so much, Mr Carton.

CARTON

Please don't thank me. I can assure you I'm ashamed of myself for making you such a terribly meagre offering.

LUCIE

But I really love it. *(She pins it on her dress.)* Don't you think it looks well on my dress?

> CARTON *bows.* LUCIE *turns round and examines herself in the glass.*

And you haven't told me yet how you like the dress.

CARTON

(Quietly) It's very pretty.

LUCIE

(Having expected something more fulsome) Oh! *(Rather coldly)* Shall I get you some wine, Mr Carton?

CARTON

(Bowing) Please. Then I can drink to your happiness.

> *He watches her smiling, as she goes to a decanter, pours him out a glass and hands it to him.*

You're angry with me, aren't you?

LUCIE

Angry with you?

CARTON

Because I didn't say that your wedding dress was the most beautiful thing I had ever seen.

LUCIE

You said it was very pretty.

CARTON

Yes. *(He raises his glass.)* To your very great happiness, Miss Manette. *(He drinks.)* Tell me, Miss Manette, am I very disagreeable to you?

LUCIE

Of course not. Why ever should you think so?

CARTON

I have it on good authority that I am. Tell me, though, honestly, am I boorish and rude and altogether unbearable?

LUCIE

Well, you are a little ungracious sometimes. Tell me, why do you profess to hate the world and everything in it?

CARTON

I never profess anything of the sort.

LUCIE

Indifference is far worse. One can't go through life without emotion or feeling for anything.

CARTON

(Shortly) One can try. I hope one can succeed.

LUCIE

I often think about you, Mr Carton, and when I do, I'm usually very troubled.

CARTON

(With an imitation of STRYVER*)* That must be the worst of my long list of crimes—that I should trouble anyone as fair and charming as yourself. *(Smiling)*

   A distant roll of thunder.

LUCIE

Have you no ambition at all?

CARTON

Yes. To serve you, Miss Manette.

LUCIE

Oh, please be serious. Have you no ambition to succeed in your profession?

CARTON

I leave that to the Stryvers of this world. I despise my profession.

LUCIE

Then why follow it?

CARTON

I don't know. My lodgings are conveniently near the law-courts— and almost next door to the Hoop and Toy.

   LUCIE *sighs hopelessly and turns away.*

I'm afraid this is a gloomy conversation for your wedding eve, Miss Manette. In fact I'm a gloomy person altogether. I'd better take myself off.

LUCIE

No. Please don't go.

CARTON

I must. *(He drains his glass and puts it down.)* Miss Manette, you have been very good to me. Though I may not appear grateful, I should like you to know that I am.

LUCIE

(Puzzled) I've done nothing to deserve your gratitude.

CARTON

Oh yes, you have. Believe me when I say that just to have known you has made me very happy.

LUCIE

That sounds as if you were saying goodbye.

CARTON

I am. That's why I came this evening. To wish you happiness and to say goodbye.

LUCIE

You're going away?

CARTON

Yes.

LUCIE

For ever?

CARTON

Yes.

LUCIE

But won't we ever see you again?

CARTON

I don't think so.

LUCIE

I'm so sorry.

> *There is another roll of thunder, followed by the sound of rain falling.* MISS PROSS *comes in, carrying a basket and an umbrella.*

MISS PROSS

(As she enters) Just got in in time. It'll be coming down cats and dogs in a minute. *(Seeing* CARTON*)* Well! So this is what goes on as soon as my back is turned. Ladybird, you ought to be ashamed of yourself. Really, you'd think young girls had no sense of decency nowadays.

LUCIE

But Prossie—

MISS PROSS

Don't you "Prossie" me. Do you think it's a nice way to behave, all alone here with a strange man on the night before your wedding?

LUCIE

But Mr Carton isn't a strange man, Prossie. He took the trouble to come all this way to give me a lovely wedding present, and I wasn't going to turn him out.

MISS PROSS

Mr Carton's got no more right here than a flea in a bishop's canonicals.

She snatches up the decanter and puts it away.

Come on. Out you go.

CARTON

I was just going when you came in, Miss Pross.

LUCIE

No, Mr Carton. You can't possibly leave till the storm's over. It's pouring. You'll be drenched.

CARTON

I really ought to...

LUCIE

Nonsense. I won't hear of it. You must stay until the rain stops. Don't mind Prossie. She's not nearly as fierce as she sounds.

MISS PROSS

Hm. Is that so? Let's see the present he's given you. Yes, that's nice. *(Glancing at* CARTON*)* I've always liked that brooch.

LUCIE

How do you mean you've always liked it?

MISS PROSS

What I say. There's one thing, it suits you a good deal better than it suited him.

LUCIE

Oh. Oh yes, I remember now. Mr Carton, you shouldn't have done that.

CARTON

I was afraid you might recognise it. I'm sorry. I was too lazy to buy you a real present.

MISS PROSS

Too lazy? That's what you say. I know different. Borrowing money off that Jerry Cruncher person of Mr Lorry's. Oh yes, I know. And he told me something else too. You've lost your job with Mr Stryver, haven't you? Down on your uppers, that Cruncher said you were.

CARTON

Jerry Cruncher's a liar.

MISS PROSS

I shouldn't be at all surprised. But he didn't lie about this.

  CARTON *turns away impatiently.*

Oh well, I'm up to my eyes in jobs. Ladybird, remember, when the rain stops, out he goes, broke or not broke.

  MISS PROSS *goes out.*

LUCIE

Mr Carton, you said you were going away.

CARTON
I'm sorry.

LUCIE
So am I. I'm sorry that losing your job and being what Prossie calls down on your uppers should be a good reason for not coming to visit us any more.

    CARTON *says nothing.*

Why did you lose your job?

CARTON
Picked a quarrel with Stryver. I was bored with him and tired of acting as his jackal. So one night when I was drunk and he was particularly tiresome, I hit him in the face.

LUCIE
Wasn't that a very silly thing to do?

CARTON
Yes. But very satisfactory.

LUCIE
(After a pause) Will you do something for me, Mr Carton?

CARTON
If I can.

LUCIE
Find yourself another job, work like a slave, don't get drunk, don't hit your employer in the face, and start your whole life again from the beginning.

CARTON
Would that really please you?

LUCIE
Of course it would.

CARTON

You know, you make it very hard for an honest waster to call his soul his own.

LUCIE

(Eagerly) Then will you do what I ask?

CARTON

I think I'd do anything in the world that would give you pleasure. In fact, to please you I might even face the depressing prospect of taking life seriously.

LUCIE

Is that a promise?

CARTON

If it is, it's one that might easily be broken.

> *There is a distant roll of thunder. The front door bell rings.*

LUCIE

Oh. That must be Charles, at last.

MISS PROSS

(Off) What are you doing here at this time of day? No, you mustn't go in. She's in her wedding dress. Don't you know it's unlucky? Why can't you wait till tomorrow? After tonight you'll be seeing her every evening for the rest of your life.

> DARNAY *comes in, brushing the rain off his clothes. He stops, disconcerted, when he sees* CARTON. LUCIE *goes to him.*

LUCIE

Oh, poor Charles. You're soaking wet. Give me your hat and coat, and come over to the fire.

DARNAY

It's nothing. It'll soon dry. *(Taking both her hands)* Lucie, you look adorable. Carton you don't deserve this special privilege. Never mind—I don't grudge it you.

CARTON comes up to him with outstretched hand.

CARTON

Darnay, I've never had a chance to congratulate you. I'd like to do so now. *(He shakes his hand, and speaks very sincerely.)* I hope more than anything in the world that you and Miss Manette will be very happy.

DARNAY

(Surprised at the warmth in his tone) Thank you, Carton. That's very kind of you.

CARTON

(In a different tone) I seem always to be congratulating you, Mr Darnay. If it isn't because you are not going to be hanged, it's because you're going to get yourself married.

LUCIE

Tomorrow all three of us are beginning a new life. May it bring great happiness to us all.

DARNAY

What is the new life you are beginning tomorrow, Mr Carton?

CARTON

I shudder to think. But may it bring me happiness all the same.

LUCIE

Oh look! An omen. The rain has stopped. Perhaps it will be fine tomorrow after all.

She goes to the window. The two MEN follow her and stand on either side, looking out.

How quiet it always is after the rain. Except for the footsteps echoing round this old house.

They listen in silence. The footsteps are audible.

Do you know—it may seem foolish—but I've often fancied that the sounds one hears from this window are the echoes of all the footsteps that are one day coming into our lives. Charles—

She takes his hand.

CARTON

(After listening further) Then it seems as if there was a great crowd of people bearing down on us.

> *They stand silently, listening. The footsteps begin to beat in unison, suggesting a crowd on the march. The sound of a drum can distantly be heard. The lights dim. In the darkness the drum beats become louder.*
>
> *The three figures of* LUCIE, CARTON *and* DARNAY *can still be dimly seen at the window in the Soho room in the middle of the stage, but now,* MADAME DEFARGE *can be seen, standing, beating a drum. She begins to march downstage, followed at first by* DEFARGE, *then* JACQUES *and a growing crowd of men and women. They march in time like soldiers.*
>
> *They swarm forward, growing more intense in revolution fever, brandishing real and improvised weapons.*
>
> MADAME DEFARGE *leads the Crowd in song, wildly, in unison.*

MADAME DEFARGE *and the Crowd*

Allons enfants de la patrie
Le jour de gloire est arrivé—

> *The* DEFARGES *and their Crowd engulf the three figures in the Soho house, and these three transform into members of the revolution. They reach a mad and wild crescendo, then in unison exclaim in a roaring scream previously unknown to human ears.*
>
> *End of Act Two.*

ACT THREE

SCENE ONE

A room in Tellson's Bank, London. It is a few months later, December 1789. LORRY *is at his desk, sorting and arranging papers. A* CLERK *is at another desk in the corner, busily writing.* DARNAY *is talking to* LORRY.

LORRY

So you think I'm too old to come with you, eh Charles?

DARNAY

Well, I know you're the youngest man that ever lived, my dear Lorry, still I must say that a long journey in bad weather to a city disorganised by revolution—now I, young as I am, feel anxious to tackle it.

LORRY

Fiddlesticks. If Paris weren't disorganised I wouldn't be going there. That's precisely why the Bank is sending me over. You've no conception of the chaos and confusion of affairs at our Paris branch. Someone has to go there and set them to rights.

DARNAY

But, my dear friend, you forget the dangers—

LORRY

Dangers? Who's going to interfere with an old codger like me? They're so busy killing each other over there that they won't have any time to bother about an old English banker. No, Charles, don't you worry, with you for company I shall be perfectly safe. Besides, Tellson's is in danger and I've served Tellson's for fifty years.

> JERRY *comes in.*

Yes, Jerry? What is it, my good fellow?

JERRY

The coach is 'ere, sir, and I've put everything in.

LORRY

All right, Jerry. We shall be ready to leave in about five minutes. Put this up in the window, will you, while you're waiting, and then bring round the coach to the side door.

JERRY

Yes, sir.

> *Exit* JERRY.

DARNAY

Are we taking Jerry with us?

LORRY

Yes. He wanted to come so badly, I couldn't refuse him.

> *There are cries and exclamations outside as* JERRY *posts the news in the window.*

These confounded emigrés. They hang around the bank every day trying to see me to advance them money, and asking about the rumours from Paris. I put the news up in our window whenever it comes—so that they can read it without bothering me...

> CARTON *comes in. He is very ragged and decayed in appearance.*

What is it now, sir? *(Not recognising him)* I'm sorry, monsieur. I can't see anyone now. *(Calling)* Jerry!

JERRY

(Appearing at the door) I'm sorry, sir. These damned Marqueeses. It's worse than the storming of the Bastille. 'Ere, out you go, Froggy.

LORRY

Why did you let this gentleman in? I told you—

CARTON

It's my fault, Lorry. Don't blame Jerry.

LORRY

God bless my soul, Mr Carton. All right, Jerry.

> JERRY *goes.*

Well, this is a surprise. How are you? *(Shaking hands)* I didn't recognise you at first.

CARTON

Am I so much changed?

LORRY

(Tactfully) No, no. Hardly at all. But you must remember that I haven't seen you now for—let me see now—why, it must have been half a year. Where have you been hiding yourself all this time?

CARTON

Oh, one place and another. How are you, Darnay?

DARNAY

(Coldly) Thank you, Mr Carton, very well.

CARTON

And your wife?

DARNAY

Very well, thank you. *(He turns his back and walks away.)*

LORRY

(Distressed at DARNAY's attitude) I am so sorry you should have chosen just this moment to come and see me, because Charles and I are in the throes of departure. We are leaving for Paris in a few minutes' time. I do hope you'll come round one day after I come back. *(Putting on his coat)*

CARTON

(Shrugging his shoulders) Oh, of course. I'm sorry to have disturbed you when you're busy. I'll be off—unless, you'd allow me to speak to you privately for a moment, Darnay.

DARNAY

(Glancing at LORRY*)* Is it important? Lorry and I have to leave almost at once if we are to get to Dover in time.

LORRY

You can have a few minutes, Charles. I'll wait for you in the coach. *(To* CLERK*)* My passport, please.

> The CLERK *gives it to him.*

Good-bye, Carton. Don't forget to visit me when I return. Don't be too long, Charles.

> LORRY *goes out.*

DARNAY

Well, Carton, what is it you wish to say to me?

CARTON

(Hesitant and embarrassed) Let's leave that for the moment. Tell me, why are you going to France?

DARNAY

If it is any business of yours, sir, I am going to give evidence at the trial of a friend of mine who is in prison.

CARTON

I see. The call of duty, is that it? What is this man to you that his being in prison should make you go scampering off to France at a moment's notice?

DARNAY

Monsieur Gabelle is the servant of my uncle, the Marquis de St. Evrémonde, who was murdered in France last year—

CARTON

Really! I had no idea you were related to that old monster. I beg your pardon for speaking so disrespectfully about your deceased relative. Please go on.

DARNAY

Monsieur Gabelle is also the family agent. He is responsible for paying me a small legacy every year. Now he writes that this fact has been discovered and he has been thrown into prison on my account. He begs me to come to Paris and help to free him.

CARTON

It'll be dangerous for you in France, you know.

DARNAY

I don't agree with you. And anyway, if you imagine that a possible slight danger for myself is going to stop me trying to save the life of an old servant, you're quite mistaken.

CARTON

Very noble of you, I'm sure. All the same I wouldn't go if I were you.

DARNAY

No, Mr Carton. Probably you wouldn't.

CARTON

I was thinking of your wife.

DARNAY

My wife is none of your business, sir.

CARTON

No, I suppose not. *(Pause)* Is she very angry with me?

DARNAY

I don't think she has any feelings about you now, Mr Carton. After all, we've not seen you for many months. She was deeply distressed by the stories she was constantly hearing of your activities. Now I think—in fact I hope—she has forgotten all about you.

CARTON

I should never have made her that promise. I warned her I'd probably break it.

A pause. DARNAY *considers* CARTON.

DARNAY

(He takes out his wallet and gives CARTON *some money.)* Find yourself some decent occupation and buy yourself some new clothes and any other things you need.

CARTON

You're very good.

DARNAY

Promise me not to disappear again and spend the next few days in the Hoop and Toy.

CARTON

I promise, but of course, I'm rather apt to break my promises, you know.

DARNAY

For heaven's sake, man, make an effort to keep this one. It's not too late. It never is.

CARTON

Perhaps. I'd like to keep it.

DARNAY

Well, I must go. *(To* CLERK*)* Is my passport ready?

CLERK

Yes, sir. I made it out in the name of St. Evrémonde, as you said, occupation, school-teacher.

DARNAY

Yes. That's right. Well, Carton, good-bye and good luck.

CARTON
Good-bye.

DARNAY *goes out.*

And good luck. Clerk?

CLERK
Yes sir?

CARTON
We live in troublesome times.

CLERK
We do indeed sir.

CARTON
And you, I expect, are the first man in England to hear of the troubles across the water.

CLERK
Yes I expect so, sir. We have messages from France almost every hour.

A message arrives. The CLERK *reads it out aloud*

"A new law has been tabled in the French Convention called the Law of Suspects. If it is passed all noblemen and all relatives and dependants of noblemen will be liable to arrest at sight."

CARTON
Arrest at sight?

CLERK
Yes, sir. I thank my stars I am safe in England.

CARTON *begins counting the money* DARNAY *has given him.*

CARTON
What is the price of a passage to France?

CLERK
Well, sir, it depends.

CARTON
(Showing the CLERK *all the money Darnay gave him*) Will that pay for it?

CLERK
(Counting) Oh yes, sir.

CARTON
Book me a passage for tomorrow night, and can you get a passport for me, too? The name is Sydney Carton.

CLERK
Sydney Carton. Yes, sir. *(Writing)* Description...yes—age?

CARTON
Twenty-seven, Gentlemen, shall we say?

CARTON *goes out.*

End of scene.

Scene Two

LORRY'S *lodgings in Paris.*

The room is on the first floor, with windows at the back of it. The red glow of a fire in the street outside and wild shouts and singing can be heard. LORRY *is writing at a desk in the room when there is a violent knocking at the front door.* MISS PROSS *comes downstairs from the second floor, carrying a candle.*

MISS PROSS

(Calling behind her up the stairs) Where's that Cruncher? Cruncher!

There is no reply.

LORRY

(Calling) What is it, Miss Pross?

MISS PROSS

(Opening the door and looking in from the landing) Someone at the door.

She begins to exit; the knocking is repeated.

(Calling) All right. I'm coming.

LORRY

(coming onto the landing; urgently) Be careful. It might be those people in the street. I'd better go.

MISS PROSS

(Sharply) You stay here. I'm more of a match for these shameless creatures than you are. *(As she passes the landing window)* Look at them—the wicked French hussies. Dancing about in the street like that! It's disgusting.

> *Knocking is repeated, louder.*

(Calling) I'm coming. I'm coming.

> MISS PROSS *screams. She then appears, supporting* LUCIE, *who is hardly able to walk.*

MISS PROSS

Ladybird! My darling. My darling. Why did you go out? Where have you been?

LORRY

(Running down to meet them) Lucie, my child! Thank God you're safe in English lodgings. Miss Pross, get the cognac.

> *They support her in to the room, and put her in a chair.*

What have you been doing? We thought you were safely in bed, asleep.

LUCIE

(Shuddering) Those terrible women! I had to fight my way through them. Some of them had blood on their faces—*(She cries on his shoulder.)*

LORRY

My poor child. My poor child. It was madness to go out. If I'd known I'd never have let you go alone.

> MISS PROSS *brings a glass of cognac.*

MISS PROSS

There, my darling. There. Drink this.

> LUCIE *sips the brandy.*

There, my precious.

LUCIE

Thank you both. It was those women—*(Smiling shamefacedly)* I'm not very brave, am I?

MISS PROSS

(Back in her usual manner) Quite brave enough, if you ask me. Not content with following that precious husband of yours to this wicked city—you must needs go gallivanting all by yourself for a little jaunt around the town.

> *She takes the glass from* LUCIE.

LUCIE

I went to Gabelle's trial. *(She shudders)* I wish I hadn't now. It's something I shall never forget as long as I live.

LORRY

Don't tell us, my dear, if it upsets you.

LUCIE

If I'd been able to stand with Charles and Father, I would not have cared so much, but they were among the witnesses, far away on the other side of the court. They were not allowed to speak, although their evidence would have proved that poor Gabelle was innocent. It was horrible—the crowd yelling for blood and those mad judges shouting and ringing a bell. Oh, God! *(She hides her face, shuddering.)*

LORRY

Then—Gabelle?

LUCIE

What chance had he got? I couldn't bear to wait for the verdict, but there could only have been one.

MISS PROSS

They're a pack of stinking murderers. That's all they are.

LUCIE

(Continuing after a pause) When I came out of the court, I was in a panic and I thought there were two men following me, I could hear their footsteps behind me all the way home. And then—those women!

> MISS PROSS *goes to the window and looks out.*

LORRY

My poor child! No wonder you were frightened.

MISS PROS

(At window) Ladybird—those men you thought were following you; what did they look like?

LUCIE

One was wearing a big top-coat with a turned-up collar, and they both had those cockades.

MISS PROSS

Then they're down there now, watching this house.

LORRY

(Sharply) What?

> *He and* LUCIE *run to the window.*

MISS PROSS

Look! Down there! Skulking in that corner.

LUCIE

Yes. Those are the men.

MISS PROSS

(Suddenly pushing LUCIE *back)* Get back. One of them has seen us. He's coming towards the front door.

> *There is a knocking at the front door.* MISS PROSS *runs to the landing.*

LORRY

Don't go, Prossie! Where's Jerry? *(Calling)* Jerry!

> JERRY *appears with a blunderbuss.*

JERRY

Yes, sir?

LORRY

There's a man trying to break into our lodgings—

JERRY

Oh, is there just? I knows 'ow to deal with these froggies.

> JERRY *goes to the door, just as* CARTON *enters.* CARTON *is wearing a revolutionary cockade.*

(*Levelling the blunderbuss at* CARTON) 'Ere now, Mounseer, out you go. We don't want no revolution in 'ere, thank you very much. Come on, out!

CARTON

All right, Jerry. You can drop that little toy of yours.

JERRY

(*Starting back*) Lord save us!

> LORRY *and* LUCIE *utter exclamations of surprise.* JERRY *follows* CARTON *into the room.*

CARTON

(*Entering the room*) Don't be alarmed, please. I'm no apparition. Sydney Carton in the flesh.

LORRY

Carton—what in the name of God are you doing in Paris?

CARTON

Ah. That is rather difficult to answer. Having a look round, shall we say?

LORRY

(*Bitterly*) I don't know if you realise, sir, that these are my lodgings—

CARTON

I realise that perfectly, sir. Something about me distresses you, eh? You usen't to talk like that in London. I suppose it's this little emblem of mine.

> *He indicates the cockade, then turns to* LUCIE *and speaks in a different tone.*

Mrs Darnay, if you love your husband you must see that he leaves Paris tonight.

LUCIE

Why are you trying to frighten me like this, Mr Carton? Or should I call you Citizen Carton?

CARTON

Charles is in danger of being denounced as a nobleman and traitor to the Republic.

LUCIE

Impossible.

CARTON

Only too possible, unless he leaves Paris at once.

LUCIE

Charles has renounced his title and supports the Republic. Who would denounce him?

CARTON

He has an enemy—

LUCIE

(Staring straight at CARTON*)* That may well be.

CARTON

...who demands his life. *(Turning to* JERRY*)* Jerry, will you please have the goodness to let in the man you will find standing at the front door?

JERRY

(Looking doubtfully at LORRY*)* What about it, sir?

LORRY

If this is treachery, Carton—

CARTON *shrugs his shoulders.*

LUCIE

Let that man in, Jerry.

Still carrying the blunderbuss, JERRY *goes out, downstairs.* MISS PROSS *makes a move to follow him.*

No, stay here, Prossie.

MISS PROSS

Well, I must say these are pretty queer goings-on, even for Paris. I can tell you I, for one, won't be happy till I'm back in London, where it's possible to see a few faces that don't glare mid-night murder and mischief at you. I haven't taken at all kindly to these foreigners. I'm a subject of His Gracious Majesty, King George the Third, God bless him, and my maxim is confound their politics, frustrate their knavish tricks, on him our hopes we fix, God save the King.

BARSAD *enters.*

BARSAD

Good evening, all.

LORRY

Hello, you are English, aren't you? Wait a moment, I recognise you, where have I seen you before?

BARSAD

Nowhere, you fool!

LORRY

That's right, I recognise you from the Old Bailey—Charles Darnay's trial, you appeared as a witness for the prosecution. May I ask, what name did you go by then?

CARTON

Barsad. May I take the liberty of presenting the gentleman to the company.

MISS PROSS

I'm sure I don't want to meet your precious friend. And as for liberty,
I've had enough of that these last few days to last me a lifetime.

>   MISS PROSS *exits*

CARTON

Quite so. I'm not sure I'm not finding it a bit tedious myself.

LORRY

Carton, how dare you bring this fellow here?

CARTON

You know, Lorry, you mustn't insult Mr Barsad. He is a person of
great importance here in Paris.

BARSAD

Agent for the Committee of Public Safety.

CARTON

Why use the longer word? One may almost think you were ashamed
to be a spy for our glorious Revolution.

LUCIE

Mr Carton, I beg you to come to the matter which brought you
here. You say Charles's life is in danger.

CARTON

Mr Barsad, whose business it is to know everything that goes
on in this city, told me of this danger an hour ago. I offered him
immediately one thousand louis if he could get both of you out of
the country tonight.

LORRY

Your revolutionary activities must be very profitable, Mr Carton. A
thousand louis is a large sum.

CARTON

I offered it in your name, of course.

>   LUCIE *stares at him, then laughs.*

LUCIE

I hope you are going to get the larger share, Mr Carton. Five hundred louis seem hardly fair, considering the trouble you have been put to.

> CARTON *clenches his fist and then shrugs his shoulders carelessly.*

CARTON

Give me those passports, Barsad.

> BARSAD *hands papers to* CARTON.

They need your seal.

BARSAD

Is the money all right?

CARTON

Yes.

LUCIE

Don't you think it is time we stopped this ridiculous game?

CARTON

Don't listen to her. I'll see that you get your money.

BARSAD

What happens if I don't?

CARTON

Something very unpleasant—to me, I imagine, citizen. Come on.

> *He has made a seal on the paper and holds it out to* BARSAD, *who grins and presses his ring on paper.*

Good. Now for Darnay.

> *He is holding out the other passport for* BARSAD, *when there is a sudden loud knocking at the front door.*

VOICE

(*Off*) Open in the name of the Republic.

Panic in the room.

CARTON

(In a whisper) So soon. Oh, God!

LUCIE

(Hysterically to CARTON*)* It is you—it is you who betrayed him.

CARTON

You believe that?

> *There is a noise of many voices as the front door is burst open. A* CROWD *of ragged men and women, headed by* MADAME DEFARGE, *invade the staircase and the landing.* MADAME DEFARGE *enters the room. As in Act 1 Scene 3, the audience are the jury during* MADAME DEFARGE*'s trial of* MDARNAY. MISS PROSS *shoulders her way through the crowd to protect* LUCIE. MADAME DEFARGE *slowly approaches* LUCIE *and stares at her coldly.*

DEFARGE

Where is the Citizen Evrémonde?

LUCIE

We know no one of that name.

DEFARGE

Do not lie to me, citizeness. Where is Charles Evrémonde, known as Charles Darnay, aristocrat and traitor?

LUCIE

My husband is no traitor.

> DEFARGE *goes to find* DARNAY.

MADAME DEFARGE

That is for the tribunal to decide. Answer me, citizeness. Where is your husband?

> *Before* LUCIE *can answer,* DARNAY *has come up the stairs, and has shouldered his way through the crowd, followed by* DR MANETTE.

DARNAY

Who asks for me?

MADAME DEFARGE

(Turning) Charles Evrémonde, once Marquis de St. Evrémonde, I arrest you in the name of the Republic.

DARNAY

What am I accused of?

MADAME DEFARGE

Of being an aristocrat and a traitor. Take him away.

LUCIE

(Wildly) No, no. He has done nothing. You can't take him!

> LUCIE *runs to* DR MANETTE.

(Hysterically) Father, save him. They are going to kill him!

DR MANETTE

Who are my son-in-law's accusers?

MADAME DEFARGE

Myself and my husband are two of his accusers. Ernest and Thérèse Defarge. You don't remember me?

DR MANETTE

No. No. I don't remember your face. That part of my life is a blank, but at least I remember the name. And you must remember me— Alexandre Manette, your husband's old master?

> MADAME DEFARGE *laughs.*

And your old friend.

MADAME DEFARGE

(To the Crowd) Take him away.

DR MANETTE

No, no, stop. I demand to know why you are denouncing my son-in-law.

MADAME DEFARGE
You ask me that?

DR MANETTE
I do.

MADAME DEFARGE
You'll know soon enough.

DR MANETTE
I demand to know now.

MAN
Who are you to demand, citizen?

DR MANETTE
I have suffered for the Republic in a way that none of you can have done—patriots as you are. For twenty years I was a prisoner in the Bastille.

MAN
(To MADAME DEFARGE*)* Is that true?

MADAME DEFARGE
Yes, quite true.

DR MANETTE
And I tell you that this woman is lying when she says my son-in-law is a traitor. I can personally testify that long before the Revolution he voluntarily renounced all his titles, wealth and possessions for the sake of the people.

WOMAN
How about that? That's a lie, isn't it?

MADAME DEFARGE
No, again quite true.

MAN

(*Releasing his hold on* DARNAY) Then I'd like to know why you're denouncing this man, son-in-law of a Bastille prisoner?

There is a murmur of agreement from the other revolutionaries.

MADAME DEFARGE

My husband and I are not alone. There is one other.

MAN

Who is he?

MADAME DEFARGE

Dr Alexandre Manette.

DR MANETTE *puts his hand to his head.*

DR MANETTE

The citizeness is mad, my friends.

MADAME DEFARGE

I repeat, Dr Alexandre Manette—formerly prisoner in the Bastille—accuses the Citizen of Evrémonde formerly Marquis de St. Evrémonde—of being an enemy of the people. Dr Manette, tell the citizeness by whom you were thrown into the Bastille. And why.

DR MANETTE

No. (*Whispering*) I shan't tell.

MADAME DEFARGE

(*Pointing to the paper in his hand*) Dr Manette, is this your writing?

DR MANETTE *looks at it and then with a low moan tries to seize it but fails.*

MADAME DEFARGE

Citizens, let me tell you how this document came into my hands. When the Bastille was taken we searched the cell where Dr Manette had been imprisoned, No. 105, North Tower. Isn't that correct, Doctor?

DR MANETTE *sinks into a chair, his head in his hands.*

The crowd which has been commenting and chattering grows suddenly silent.

Under a stone in the cell was found this paper. It was known to be there because the doctor in his raving had told what he had written and where he had hidden it. Will you read it, Doctor?

MADAME DEFARGE *gives it to him.*

DR MANETTE
No. No.

He drops the paper. LUCIE *picks it up.*

MADAME DEFARGE
Then you read it, citizeness.

MAN
What is in the paper? What does it say?

LUCIE
"I, Alexandre Manette, do solemnly declare that I am in possession of my right mind, and that everything I here set down is the truth.

One night in December, 1767, a carriage drew up at the door of my house. A young man of quality stepped out, and asked me to go with him in his coach to attend an urgent case. We drove out of the town to a large white château; I was conducted to an upper chamber and there I found a patient in a high fever of the brain, a young woman of not more than twenty. There was little to be done for here, but all that was possible I did. After about an hour she died."

DR MANETTE
My darling, my darling, forgive me—

LUCIE
"The young nobleman told me to come with him into another room, where I would find a second patient—a mere boy of not less than seventeen, dying of a rapier thrust through the lung.

The boy and the girl were brother and sister. The young nobleman who had brought me up to the château had seen her and desired her, and had demanded his rights of her. Though she refused him, he had borne off the girl to his château. But the brother had gone straight to the château and attacked the young nobleman. In the presence of his sister the boy had been mortally wounded, and now lay dying at my feet. Before he died he begged me to take care of the one remaining member of the family—his second sister.

I went at once to the cottage where the boy had told me I would find his other sister. The cottage was empty and she was gone.

On returning home I immediately drew up a report of all that I had seen and heard in this nobleman's château. This report I forwarded to the Minister of France. A week later my servant admitted to my house two men clothed in black who brought me to the Bastille."

> LUCIE *drops the letter and clasps her father, sobbing, while* MADAME DEFARGE *picks it up and continues reading.*

MADAME DEFARGE

"The name of the nobleman to whose house I went on that night and who procured the *lettre de cachet* which has consigned me to oblivion, is St. Evrémonde—the Marquis de St. Evrémonde. And him and his descendants, to the last of their race, I, Alexandre Manette, unhappy prisoner, do this last night of the year 1777, in my unbearable agony, denounce to the times when all these things will be answered for. Arrest him!"

> DARNAY *is taken.* LUCIE *clasps her father in her arms, sobbing. There is a shout of hate from the crowd, they dance and shake their fists.* DARNAY *is surrounded and dragged to the door. They spit at him.* DR MANETTE *is sunk in apathy.* LUCIE *rushes forward.*

LUCIE

No, no, you mustn't take him. Charles had nothing to do with that.

MADAME DEFARGE

His name is Evrémonde.

LUCIE

(Wildly) Then so is mine. He's no more guilty than I am. *(Kneeling at* MADAME DEFARGE'S *feet)* Don't let them do this. You must

have some pity even if they have none. You're a woman. You must know what I'm suffering.

MADAME DEFARGE

(*Raising her hand for silence*) Save your words, citizeness. Dr Manette, you prayed to God that the sister of that murdered boy and girl might be alive today. You see her here.

> *She looks down at* LUCIE *and then turns to the door.* MADAME DEFARGE *marches triumphantly down the stairs, followed by* DARNAY *who is guarded by the crowd. The crowd laughs, hoots and screams as they leave. The front door slams, and we hear them singing and yelling as they go down the street.*

LUCIE

He will perish—there is no real hope.

CARTON

Yes, he will perish. There is no real hope.

> *He crosses the room and looks at himself curiously in the glass.*

> *End of scene.*

Scene Three

A corner of a wine shop in Paris.

Only a fireplace and a table can be seen. CARTON *sits alone. A bottle is on the table by him, but the glass at his side is untouched. A figure appears behind him, and squints down over* CARTON'S *shoulder.* CARTON *starts and looks up. It is* BARSAD. CARTON *hastily takes up a paper which lies on the table before him, and pockets a hand-mirror which he has been studying.*

CARTON

What the devil are you doing here?

BARSAD

Thank God, I've found you. Lucky I remembered you always come to this place.

CARTON

What do you want?

BARSAD

Listen, Carton, where's that passport I gave you for Evrémonde's wife?

CARTON

I don't know. Why?

BARSAD

You've got to give it back to me, do you hear?

CARTON

I hear. There's no need to shout. What's the trouble?

BARSAD

She's been denounced.

CARTON

What? Are you sure? Who by?

BARSAD

The Defarge woman.

CARTON

When will they come to arrest her?

BARSAD

Tomorrow, I expect. Maybe tonight. If they find her gone they'll want to know how she got out of Paris, and then—So you see you'd better give it back to me if you value your skin.

A pause. CARTON *makes no move.*

(Threateningly) I can very easily make you give it back, you know. One word from me, and—*(He makes an expressive gesture.)*

CARTON

Yes, I see. Sit down, Barsad, and have a glass of brandy. I'm going to have a talk with you.

BARSAD

I haven't got time to listen to you now.

CARTON

Don't worry. I won't let Madame Defarge catch you here. *(Meaningly)* I won't let her catch you at all if you're reasonable. Sit down.

BARSAD *sits unwillingly.* CARTON *pours out two glasses of brandy.*

BARSAD

Look here, what's the game?

CARTON

A winning game for me. I hold all the cards, Barsad. First, I know your real name. What do you call yourself over here, by the way? Barsad? Sheep of the prisons? Turnkey? Spy? Secret informer?

BARSAD

Never mind.

CARTON

Oh, well, it doesn't matter. My second card is—I know what you were before you became a supporter of the French Republic. You were a spy in the pay of an aristocratic government. Isn't that correct? You may have been other things beside, but that is enough.

BARSAD

I don't know what you're driving at.

CARTON

Have a little patience. This is my third card. You're afraid of Madame Defarge. She's knitted your name in the register.

BARSAD

How do you know?

CARTON

I do know. And now my ace. (*He takes a sip of brandy.*) Denunciation of Mr Barsad to the nearest Section Committee as a spy, conveniently led by the incomparable woman, Madame Defarge, and a subsequent but certain appointment with the guillotine. Now look over *your* hand, Mr Barsad, and see what you hold. Don't hurry.

BARSAD

You wouldn't do that, you wouldn't denounce me to that woman?

CARTON

You scarcely seem to like your hand, Mr Barsad. Do I win?

BARSAD *is silent and stares at* CARTON.

CARTON

(Rising) Very well, I shall go down to St. Antoine and play my ace. You may expect visitors at your lodging tonight.

There is a pause.

BARSAD

(Suddenly) Get her out of Paris, it's my death if she's caught.

CARTON

Exactly. And that would be a pity, wouldn't it?

LORRY *enters in cloak and hat.* BARSAD *makes a move to go.*

Don't go. I haven't finished with you yet. *(Rising to meet* LORRY*)* Thank you, Lorry. It's good of you to come.

He helps him on to the settle. LORRY *is plainly overcome with anxiety and grief.*

Well? Is the trial over?

LORRY

There was no chance—no chance without Dr Manette.

CARTON

Why didn't he go?

LORRY'S *look answers* CARTON'S *question.*

When is it to be?

LORRY

Tomorrow at dawn.

He buries his face in his hands. CARTON *rises and draws* BARSAD *aside.*

CARTON

(Aside to BARSAD*)* Now, Barsad, I'll tell you one thing that you're going to do for me. What prison is Darnay in?

BARSAD

Conciergerie. But don't ask me to get him out, because that's impossible.

CARTON

What about getting me in?

BARSAD

What do you mean?

CARTON

A last visitor before he goes to the guillotine.

BARSAD

Impossible.

CARTON

Are you sure?

BARSAD

Well, not impossible, but damned dangerous for both of us.

CARTON

That's a different matter. It can be done and anything you can do, Mr Barsad, you're going to do. Otherwise—you understand me, don't you? I'll meet you here at midnight tonight. *Au revoir.*

> BARSAD *scowls and goes out.*

LORRY

What were you saying to that man?

CARTON

Nothing much. I have gained access to Charles.

LORRY

But access to him will not save him.

CARTON

I never said it would.

A pause.

Here is Lucie's passport. *(He gives it to* LORRY.*)* And here are the Doctor's, your own, and lastly, mine.

He hands them to LORRY.

LORRY

Why yours?

CARTON

It will be safer with you. Have you made arrangements about the coach for tonight?

LORRY

Yes. I am afraid, though, she will not leave until all is over.

CARTON

(Urgently) She must. You must make her. If you delay, even until dawn, all will be lost. Have the coach wait a hundred yards down the street from the Conciergerie Prison. At half an hour past midnight, I shall come to you. Immediately I am in the coach, drive off. Any delay, any attempt to save the life of the prisoner in the Conciergerie will be fatal. Do you understand?

LORRY *gazes at him, and then nods his head dismally.*

Good.

A pause.

Please don't tell her of this interview, or this arrangement. And don't speak to her of me. I can help her without that. How does she look?

LORRY

Unhappy beyond measure. But still very beautiful.

A pause.

CARTON

(Suddenly) Yours has been a long life, Lorry, hasn't it?

LORRY

(Looking up, surprised at the change in CARTON'S *tone)* Why yes, yes. I am in my seventieth year.

CARTON

How strange it must be to look back upon a life that has been so useful. It must make you happy. And now, at seventy, you have made a place for yourself, that many people will miss when you have gone.

LORRY

A solitary old bachelor! There is nobody to weep for me.

CARTON

How can you say that? Wouldn't she weep for you?

LORRY

Yes, yes, thank God. I didn't quite mean what I said.

CARTON

It is a thing to thank God for, isn't it.

LORRY

It is, Carton, it is.

    A pause.

CARTON

I should like to ask you—does your childhood seem a long way off?

LORRY

Twenty years ago it did seem a long way off, but at this time of life, no. As I draw nearer and nearer to the end I seem to travel as if in a circle, nearer and nearer to the beginning. The way is smoothed for one. *(With a smile)* Growing old is not so very terrible. But you are still young.

CARTON

Yes. I am still young.

He raises his glass to drink, looks at it, and puts it down, untouched. Then he rises.

Come. We both of us have work to do. You must go back to your lodgings, and make all preparations for the journey.

LORRY *rises painfully,* CARTON *assisting him.*

Four is the utmost that the coach can carry. Jerry and Miss Pross must follow as best they can and meet you, please God, in Calais.

LORRY

Then you are not coming as far as Calais yourself?

CARTON

(Impatiently) Of course. I meant—meet US in Calais. Good-bye, Lorry. *(He takes his hand.)* Do not laugh at me if I say that knowing you has meant much to me.

LORRY

I am afraid it is you who are laughing at me.

CARTON

(Sincerely) Heaven forbid. Good-bye.

LORRY *turns to go.*

And—please remember . Do not speak of me to her.

LORRY

Very well. I am afraid I shall never understand you, Carton. Good-bye.

He goes out. CARTON *puts on his topcoat and hat, throws a coin on to the table and follows* LORRY *out.*

End of scene.

Scene Four

MR LORRY'S *lodgings. Night.*

The room is tidy, but empty, as if people were packed to leave it. LUCIE *and* LORRY *lead the* DOCTOR *down the stairs from the top landing. He mutters to himself.* MISS PROSS *and* JERRY *are carrying luggage from above.*

DR MANETTE

(At the landing, looking through the open door into the room) Where is my bench? I have been looking everywhere for my bench and can't find it. What have they done with my work? Time presses. I must finish those shoes.

LUCIE *and* LORRY *lead* DR MANETTE *past the room, then down the stairs to the front door. They are followed by* JERRY. MISS PROSS *packs the luggage alone.* MADAME DEFARGE *appears.*

MADAME DEFARGE

(At length) Where is the wife of Evrémonde?

Silence—MISS PROSS' *look could kill.*

Where is the wife of Evrémonde?

MISS PROSS

You might be the wife of Lucifer from your appearance. But you shan't get the better of me. I'm an Englishwoman.

MADAME DEFARGE

Go tell the wife of Evrémonde that I wish to see her. Do you hear?

MISS PROSS

If those eyes of yours were bed winches and I was an English four-poster they shouldn't loose a splinter of me. No, you wicked foreign woman, I'm your match.

MADAME DEFARGE

Woman, imbecile, pig. I take no answer from you. I demand to see her. Either tell her that I demand to see her or stand out of my way and let me go to her.

MISS PROSS

I'm a Briton, and I'm desperate. I don't care an English tuppence for myself, but I'll not leave a handful of that dark hair on your head if you lay a finger on me.

MADAME DEFARGE

You poor wretch, what are you worth? *(Shouting)* Citizen Doctor. Wife of Evrémonde. Citizen Lorry. Any person but this miserable fool answer the Citizeness Defarge.

> *There is a pause.*

This room is in disorder. There's been packing in this house. Has she gone? Answer me, has she gone?

MISS PROSS

(Darting to the main door) No, no. She is asleep upstairs. You mustn't disturb her.

MADAME DEFARGE

There is no one in the rooms upstairs. Let me look.

MISS PROSS

(Screaming) Never, never, never!

MADAME DEFARGE

If she is gone she can easily be pursued and brought back. She must not cheat the guillotine. Let me see those other rooms.

MISS PROSS

God give me strength, give me strength.

> MADAME DEFARGE *goes for the door.* MISS PROSS *holds her round the waist. They struggle.* MADAME DEFARGE *feels for her pistol.*

It's under my arm. You shan't use it. I'll hold you until one of us dies.

> MADAME DEFARGE *jerks the pistol free.* MISS PROSS *makes a despairing grab for it. The pistol goes off and* MADAME DEFARGE *sinks slowly to the floor at* MISS PROSS' *feet.* MISS PROSS *looks down at her dazed, half-sobbing.*

> JERRY *comes hastily upstairs from the front door and calls impatiently to her.*

JERRY

Miss Pross? Miss Pross? Ah, there you are, miss. Are you ready to go?

MISS PROSS

(Still dazed, on the landing) What did you say?

JERRY

(Coming closer) I only asked if you were ready to go, miss? The coach is 'ere.

MISS PROSS

Speak up, man. I can see your lips moving but I can't hear a word you say. What are you mumbling for? Oh my Lord, I can't hear my own voice. There was a flash and a crash and now everything's still. Quite, quite still. I feel I shall never hear anything again.

JERRY

(Putting his arm around her) You can't have gone deaf in these few minutes, miss. Wot's come over you? Hark! There's the roll of those dreadful carts! You can hear that, miss?

> MISS PROSS *watches his mouth and shakes her head. He helps her and they begin to descend the stairs.* MISS PROSS *looks back from time to time over her shoulder.*

> *End of scene.*

SCENE FIVE

A small cell in the Conciergerie Prison. Music plays.

CARTON *arrives and instructs* DARNAY *to swap jackets, then to write a letter as he dictates, leaning on his back.* CARTON *then places a prepared rag over* DARNAY'S *mouth and he passes out.* BARSAD *enters and puts* DARNAY *over his shoulders, takes the note from* CARTON *and says goodbye to* CARTON. BARSAD *carries the unconscious* DARNAY *to the coach and hands the note to* LUCIE *and says goodbye.* CARTON *is left alone in the cell, waiting execution. The jacket that* DARNAY *had been wearing, now worn by* CARTON, *has been marked with a large red painted cross on the back. This is the mark that the prisoner will be executed.*

The lights dim in the cell. There is a roll of drums. The inside of a coach is seen on the left of the stage. In it are LORRY *and the* DOCTOR. LUCIE *is on the back seat clasping* CARTON'S *letter, with* DARNAY—*still unconscious—resting his head on her lap. The coach stops moving and there is the sound of voices.*

LORRY
The barrier.

GUARD 1 *sticks his head through the window.*

GUARD 1
Who goes here? Who's within there? Your papers.

The papers are handed out.

Alexandre Manette. Physician. French. Which is he?

LORRY *points to* DR MANETTE *who is muttering and shaking his head.*

The citizen-doctor is not in his right mind. Lucie—his daughter. French. Where is she?

LORRY *points to* LUCIE.

Lucie—the wife of Evrémonde, is it not? Hah. Evrémonde has an appointment elsewhere today. Sydney Carton. Advocate. English. Which is he?

LORRY *points to* DARNAY.

The English advocate is in a swoon.

LORRY
He will recover in the fresh air. He has just parted from a friend who is under sentence of death.

GUARD 1
Is that all the trouble? That's nothing. Many have to look through the little window these days. You are Jarvis Lorry.

LORRY
I am.

GUARD 1
Here are your papers, Jarvis Lorry, countersigned.

LORRY
We may depart, citizen?

GUARD 1
You may depart. A good journey.

LORRY
I salute you, citizen.

The coach begins to move. The GUARD'S *head disappears.*

The first danger past. Through the barrier. Courage, my darling child—courage.

The lights dim. There is a roll of drums.

CARTON *and the* SEAMSTRESS *are facing each other.*

SEAMSTRESS

Citizen Evrémonde, do you remember? I am a poor seamstress who was with you in La Force.

CARTON

My poor child, you here!

SEAMSTRESS

I wish they had not tied my hands. While I was able to keep sowing I did not feel so frightened.

CARTON

Come closer to me, my child. It is the noise and the shouting that frightens you. Try not to listen.

SEAMSTRESS

I am not afraid to die, Citizen Evrémonde. I am glad to die if the Republic which is to do so much good to us poor will profit by my death. But I do not know how that can be. Will you tell me how that can be, Citizen Evrémonde? I am so ignorant.

CARTON

I am ignorant too, my child. I cannot tell you.

SEAMSTRESS

I was present at your trial, Citizen Evrémonde. My own followed soon after. You were very brave—an example to me. Will you come closer to me? I am not afraid, but I am weak, and it will give me more courage if you are near.

He moves close to her, and she lifts her eyes to his face. She starts back suddenly.

CARTON

Hush! Hush, my child. Say nothing.

SEAMSTRESS
Are you—are you dying for him?

CARTON
And his wife. Yes.

SEAMSTRESS
You are very brave. Will you stay by me to the last, stranger?

CARTON
Yes, stranger. To the last.

> *The lights dim. There is a roll of drums.*
>
> *The coach is seen again.*

LUCIE
Are we travelling fast enough? Surely we can go faster?

LORRY
It would seem like flight, my darling. I must not urge them too much. It would rouse suspicion.

LUCIE
Look back, look back, and see if we are pursued.

LORRY
The road is clear, my dearest. So far we are not pursued.

GUARD 2
Halt!

> *The coach stops*

LUCIE
Why have we stopped? Are we taken?

> GUARD 2's *head appears.*

GUARD 2
Answer, friends, in the carriage.

LORRY

What is it?

GUARD 2

How many did they say?

LORRY

How many?

GUARD 2

To the guillotine today? They would have told you at the last post.

LORRY

Fifty-two—they said.

GUARD 2

I said so. A brave number. My fellow-citizen here would have it forty-two. Ten more heads are worth having. Long live the guillotine! Forward, citizen, forward.

The lights dim. A roll of drums.

CARTON *and the* SEAMSTRESS *are still standing as they were when last seen.*

SEAMSTRESS

But for you, dear stranger, I should not be so composed. You have brought me great comfort. I think you were sent to me by heaven.

CARTON

And you to me. Keep your eyes on me, my child, and look at nothing else.

SEAMSTRESS

I mind nothing when you are close to me. I shall mind nothing when I leave you, if only they are quick.

CARTON

They will be quick. It will not take long.

SEAMSTRESS

You are not afraid, are you?

CARTON

Not now. Thanks to you—not now.

SEAMSTRESS

I am so happy you are with me. Otherwise I would be quite alone. I have a cousin whom I love very much. But she knows nothing of my fate. I think it is better as it is.

CARTON

Yes, yes. Better as it is.

SEAMSTRESS

And *she*? His wife? Does *she* know?

CARTON

She will know one day. I sent her a message which she will understand. I am happy thinking of her—and thinking of you.

SEAMSTRESS

They are beckoning me. Am I to kiss you now? Is the moment come?

CARTON

Yes.

> *They kiss.*

Good-bye, dear little stranger. I shall follow you very soon.

> *The* SEAMSTRESS *walks into the darkness.*

Very soon.

> *A roll of drums.*

> *The coach is seen again.* CARTON *is still visible.* LUCIE *takes the letter which she has been clasping to her breast, and reads very softly.*

LUCIE

"It is a far, far better thing that I do now than I have ever done. It is a far, far better rest that I go to now, than I have ever known."

> LUCIE *turns and identifies her husband in the coach as he regains consciousness.*

> CARTON *begins to move up the steps of the guillotine.*

> *The lights dim in the coach.*

> *A roll of drums.*

> *End.*

Lightning Source UK Ltd.
Milton Keynes UK
UKOW05f0755171013

219168UK00002B/16/P